Nice Start

Questions Only You Can Answer
to Create the Life Only You Can Live

Mark Chussil

INKWATER PRESS

Nice Start

Questions Only You Can Answer
to Create the Life Only You Can Live

www.inkwaterpress.com

ISBN-13 978-1-59299-474-8

ISBN-10 1-59299-474-1

Publisher: Inkwater Press

Printed in the U.S.A.

All paper is acid-free
and meets all ANSI standards for archival quality paper.

1 3 5 7 9 10 8 6 4 2.

This book is dedicated to my mother.
You're the greatest, and you are missed.

The covers of this book are too far apart.

Ambrose Bierce (1842-1914?)

Contents

Contents

APPENDIX 177

Introduction

You Know

You know that you have to buy a ticket if you want to win the lottery. You know that there's not some vast secret of life that can only be told now. You know that if the universe maintains an advice department, it's more likely to encourage you to take action than to recommend you sit at home and hope really hard. You know that few of the people you admire attribute their joy and success to inertia. You find it hard to imagine Captain Picard solving a galactic emergency on the starship Enterprise by commanding his crew, "Wish it so!"

You don't need someone to tell you *you can do it* and to fill you with heroic imagery of gold medals, triumphant parades, and soaring eagles. You already know, grasshopper. You've learned by experience that it works to work at something and that there's not enough time to work at everything.

You have learned much. You realize the difference between positive and negative thinking. You know the value of honesty, especially with yourself. You respect responsibility, in others and in yourself, and its power to inspire progress. You understand the strength of integrity.

What comes next, what you do with what you've learned, is up to you. That's what *Nice Start* is about and what *Nice Start* is for.

I don't know if *Nice Start* will make you happy. Of course, no book can reach into your skull and tickle your brain chemistry to cause happiness. I don't even know if you came to *Nice Start* for happiness. Maybe you came for stimulation, confirmation, clarification, education, relaxation, validation, or something else. Think about it.

"Think about it" is what *Nice Start* is about. It's about being conscious of how you think and what you think. Why is that important? Well, as they say, if you want to change your life, change your mind. *Nice Start* is about helping you consciously change your mind to get more of what you want in your life.

Nice Start is not for people who want to coast through life. It's not for people who wait for things to happen. It's not for people who want to be told what to do. It's not for people who have enough. *Nice Start* is for people who drive, who make things happen, who run their own lives, who want more. (More what? We'll get to that.) It's about deliberately, actively producing what's next in your life. It's about being conscious.

Here's an example.

A few years ago, I served as a volunteer on the staff of a personal-growth seminar. I was sitting with a group of 5 people, and we were doing an exercise in which each of us shared what we were proud of in our lives.

When it was my turn, I talked about my degrees from Yale and Harvard, the business I'd started, the book and articles I'd published, the trips around the world I'd taken, the people I loved and who loved me.

After I shared what I was proud of, I listened to comments from the group. A 15-year-old boy looked at me, smiled innocently, and said "nice start."

I was stunned. Nice *start*? Wasn't he listening? Didn't he realize how awesome my life was? He's a 15-year-old kid; what does *he* know?

I thought again… hmmm, what *does* he know?

Maybe that kid has the wisdom of the ages. Maybe he doesn't know a thing. Maybe he was being funny. Maybe he was expressing admiration and I took it as a rebuke. Whatever he thought he said, I was shaken by what I thought I heard.

Intentionally or not, he gave me a gift. His words stimulated me to compare what I had accomplished to what I want to accomplish.

I realized that I spent my days on intellectual goals and distant travel (not that there's anything wrong with that). What was missing was emotional satisfaction and sharing what I'd learned and thought. That's what I wanted next.

I changed direction. I express, not just listen. I take my time (interesting phrase). I let love into my life. I wrote this book and I'm writing another. I'm doing more big-picture public speaking and focusing my technical work on discovery. I'm living the life I've consciously chosen.

Change happens fast in the movies: Today I am a driven businessman buying low and selling high, tomorrow I am a beachcomber (what, the beaches are unruly?) permanently relaxed on an unspoiled island with the love of my life, high-speed Internet, and an all-you-can-eat coconut buffet. Real-life change may not leap like a scene transition, but it needn't dawdle either. The clearer your goal and your action, the faster you get there.

Sometimes "change" is like changing clothes: same person, new decoration. Putting on gym clothes does not make you physically fit. It doesn't even send you to the gym.

In *Nice Start* we will look at your core, not your decoration.* Like fitness, living the life you consciously choose happens by taking action and sticking to it. Imagine you've been walking in one direction and you decide to turn a little bit to the side. Perhaps you speed up to a trot or a run, too. For a while it seems you're close to the path you left. After a while, though, the old path fades from view and you are living your new life.

Nice Start is not about silver bullets, magic pills, psychobabble, too-good-to-be-true anecdotes, or be-like-me advice. It is about good questions, because good questions stimulate good answers.

Nice Start is not about my answers to those questions. I'm not wise enough, brash enough, or young enough to have your answers. It is about good questions and *your* good answers. It's your life, and it's your book now.

> **I f you don't know where you are going, any road will do.**
> Lewis Carroll (1832-1898), *Alice in Wonderland*

---

* Speaking about the core, I've wondered why people use the onion metaphor: peeling the layers of the onion to reveal what's inside, which is more onion. Seems awfully smelly to me, and it makes you cry. I prefer the artichoke metaphor: peeling the prickly leaves to get to the wonderful heart.

What's In It for You

Do people learn from experience?

Sivasailam Thiagarajan (a.k.a. Thiagi) says no, people don't learn from experience. If they did, why would we keep making the same mistakes?

People learn, Thiagi says, by reflecting on experience.

You have experience. I hope the questions in *Nice Start* help you reflect on your experience constructively and help you create consciously the life you want. Some of the questions are cheeky, some are thought-provoking, and some are bold. I intend them also to be gentle, and I find they have nuance and depth when I ponder them. Which I continue to do, because we keep discovering as long as we keep looking.

You'll find 4 sections in *Nice Start*.

Yourself. This section is all about you. Well, the whole book is. More precisely, *Yourself* is about who you are and who you want to be.

Others. The world is made up mostly of people other than you. How are others different from you, and the same as you? How do those differences and similarities affect your relationships with them? *Others* is about you and them.

Perspectives. Thinking the good old way won't bring you somewhere new. *Perspectives* is about being amused, surprised, shocked, excited, and encouraged by thinking differently. *Perspectives* is about beliefs.

Dreams. What do you dream about when you're awake? What do you want, and how will you make your dreams come true? *Dreams* is about today and tomorrow.

Another version of "what's in it for you" is "what will you get out of it." I don't know for sure what that will be; you're the one doing the getting, not me. (Was *Gone With The Wind* a love story, a war story, or an historical story? Whatever you say.) That said, here are some possibilities.

Do you wonder why people sometimes seem so ornery? You'll find explorations that may help you understand them better. (That doesn't mean you have to agree with them.) Doing Good, Irrational, The Battle of the Sexists, and They are a few of those explorations.

Do you struggle to figure out what you really want? Explorations that will interest you include Your Joy, Success, Being Marlon Brando, What's the Problem?, and One-Way Trip.

Are you vaguely disenchanted with life and wonder whether there's more? Look at explorations such as That's Life, The Briefcase, Huntington Hartford, Be Free From, and Alive.

Are you vaguely, or not so vaguely, disenchanted with how the world works? These explorations may help you perceive it differently and might even inspire you to help improve the world: Prisons, Senator, Progress, Charisma, and Utopia.

"And now a lot of words from our sponsor." What are we teaching, what are we absorbing? Although there is no escape from the commercial and cultural messages around us, that doesn't mean we have to soak them up uncritically. Look at School Today, Music, Man Loses in Casino!, Great Truths, and Believing.

Neither this book nor your life is about being grimly serious and scrunched-up proper. Have some fun! Take these explorations, please: Smile, Laugh, Acts of Kindness, and Thankful.

But wait, there's more! There are 58 explorations in *Nice Start,* and I mentioned only 28 of them. And you can ignore how I bunched them together. Go ahead, have fun with an exploration I lumped with disenchantment.

Something in *Nice Start* will save you some time or help you avoid some anguish. Something in it will help you smile or feel less alone. Something will trigger an idea, a passion, or a direction. Something will make sense, or different sense, a year from now. Something will delight you as "nice start" delighted me.

So, what's in *Nice Start* for you? Whatever you put in it. Enjoy it, and best wishes to you.

The brain can change, and that means that we can change...
If the will is there, the potential is immense.

Sharon Begley (?)

Your vision will become clear only when you look into your heart.
Who looks outside, dreams. Who looks inside, awakens.

Carl Gustav Jung (1875-1961)

Acknowledgements and Thanks

At the end of that seminar, I thanked the young man for "nice start." I hope that he sees this book and knows how powerfully he impacted my life. Alas, I don't know his name. Thank you, whoever you are.

I have many people to thank for books or seminars, for counsel and friendship, for life experiences, and for insight. Adrian Cruz, Dan Gibbons, Dave Reibstein, Dennis Damore, Ellen Potters, Elmarie Vuren, Engage Team 1, George Sousa, Joaquim Branco, Joe Bauschelt, Judith Allan, Kathy Rueda, Lois Meeth, Mark Zamkov, MLS C-58, P7 Team 336, PLD Team 5, Sidney Schoeffler, and Tom Przybylski: from my heart, thank you.

My family is wonderful. I've learned so much from them, even though at times I resisted or didn't realize I was learning. Thank you, Dad and Anne, Mom and Harry, and Paul. You are fabulous. Thanks also to Helen and Lou, James, Janice, Jean, and Ken.

Brigita, you make my heart smile. I am grateful for you every day.

Special thanks to B.U. Robert Berman, the greatest, wisest teacher of all.

Sources and Comments

I showed an early draft of *Nice Start* to my friend Dennis Damore. Some essays had explorations, some didn't. Denny suggested that I pair every essay with an exploration. That seminal idea gave the book its unifying theme.

Gina Panettieri read an early draft of the second edition and graciously gave me insightful feedback that greatly improved the book.

The personal-growth seminars to which I refer in various places were conducted by PSI Seminars and E3 Seminars. They are extraordinary.

Concepts including cognitive dissonance, confirmation bias, and overconfidence came from *Decision Traps* (J. Edward Russo and Paul J.H. Schoemaker), *Judgment in Managerial Decision Making* (Max H. Bazerman), *Mistakes Were Made (but not by me)* (Carol Tavris and Elliot Aronson), and *The Psychology of Judgment and Decision Making* (Scott Plous). The latter was especially helpful in "Reasons For." Various numerical observations came from John Allen Paulos (*Innumeracy*) and Barry Glassner (*The Culture of Fear*). The idea of "success objects" in "The Battle of the Sexists" came from books by Warren Farrell. The idea of a long list in "Time's Up" came from *The Aladdin Factor,* by Jack Canfield and Mark Victor Hansen.

I recommend Philip Zimbardo's important and unflinching book *The Lucifer Effect: Understanding Why Good People Turn Evil* (http://lucifereffect.org). You'll see related material in "Roles," "They," and elsewhere.

Almost all of the quotations in *Nice Start* were drawn from reference sites on the Internet. Dates of births and deaths came mostly from Wikipedia.org.

I use the construction "as I write these words" or the equivalent in several places. I wrote this book over several years, and I didn't write sections in the order in which they appear. So, with the exception of references to historical events, my intent is to talk about my state of mind as I wrote rather than draw a link to specific dates.

Nice Start

Yourself

If I am not for myself, who will be for me?
And when I am for myself, what am 'I'? And if not now, when?

Hillel (1st century BCE–1st century CE)

It is your responsibility to be you. Not in the sense of obligation; rather, in the sense that you are the only one who can be you.

You don't discover who you are through a series of multiple-choice questions. You don't fill out a who-you-are form, taking care to write within the lines and filing it away for future reference. You don't get it wrong, no matter who you say you are.

Who you are is how you view the world and your place in it. It is what you want, how you make decisions, what you value, what bores or excites you, what makes you get out of bed. It is what you think and how you think. It is your attitudes and assumptions.

You are complex. Like the rest of us, you see good in yourself that you wish others would see, and bad that you hope others won't see, and you wonder how the good and the bad coexist inside you. You have desires, joys, fears, and habits. Friends, family, colleagues, politicians, ads, movies, and music all tell you what you need, what you should do, and who you should be. You think *this* is who I am, and yet your feet sometimes move in a different direction. You surprise, frustrate, and delight yourself. You strive, you want, you feel, you suffer, you laugh, you love, you dream, you fall short, you rise high, and often you don't know why. You age. You live.

You are a moving target. What broke your heart or made your day at 4 is inconsequential at 40. What breaks your heart or makes your day at 40 was incomprehensible at 20. Time passes. You change. You may be surprised when you look in the mirror and into your heart.

The one thing I know about who you are is that you are human. Like the rest of us, for better or for worse. We're all in this together, and we're all doing the best we can.

Who are you now? Take a warm, kind look and notice the *you* that you have created, in all your progress, disappointment, and magnificence. What's the best about yourself? What's the worst about yourself? If you were a biographer writing about you, what would you write?

On my office walls hang pictures of me when I was a baby. I look at those pictures and I marvel at the changes. That innocent little boy, unself-conscious, full of laughter and wonder (and hair), has imperceptibly morphed into me (with less hair). Then, all was future; now, unless I defy some serious odds, most is past. I look in the mirror too: *this* is what I created from the potential in those photos. Sometimes I am proud, sometimes dismayed. I know too that I am still making choices and still creating me.

So, whoever you are, who do you want to be? There are 4 parts to the answer: point A, point B, the route from A to B, and effective action to travel that route. You don't have to brood over them in any particular order. You don't have to brood at all. It's okay to have fun. What subject could possibly be more interesting than you?

Point A. It's hard to navigate to Poughkeepsie without knowing if you are now in Peoria or Pretoria. To end at point B, you must know the point A from which you begin. So, get to know yourself. Be gently honest; there's no need to inflate or deflate. Who you are now is your point A.

You never stay at point A. You won't be the same person tomorrow that you are today. You're not the same person you were a sentence ago. I presume you consider that a good thing, because I presume that you are not hoping to be the same at the end of this book as you were when you began.

Point B. Who you want to be is point B. Be gently honest here too. Although our culture bombards you with unsubtle hints about who you should be, what matters is who *you* want to be.

The question is whether the point B you reach will be the point B you want. "What will be will be," or going wherever the universe "takes" you, will surely deliver you to *a* point B. Is it *your* point B? Only if you believe in shooting an arrow and then drawing the bullseye where it hit. So, you can deliberately select your point B, and choose your route to get there.

Your route. Nice Start doesn't assume that you want the scenic route, or the route with the fewest tolls, or the route with the smallest carbon footprint, or the route that takes you by the most shopping malls, or the route that you can travel with a bus full of friends, or the route with the most roses you can stop and smell. It doesn't even assume that there is only one point B for your whole life. It assumes only that you want to know your point A, consciously select your point B, and choose your route to get there.

Effective action. What does it take to travel all the way to point B? There is a minor industry devoted to speeches and books that encourage you to go for what you want. If you want it enough, if you absolutely, totally commit everything you've got, if you truly believe, it's yours! Wish it so. I've even heard a facilitator say "people give up just before they succeed," which is nonsensical at best and irresponsible at worst.

Those views imply that if you don't have it yet, you haven't committed or believed enough. Hmmm. As one of my teachers starkly put it, do you really believe that the people who perished on 9/11 were insufficiently committed to living?

In addition, there's what statisticians call *survivor bias*, which means the minor industry presents for our reading and listening pleasure only those people who succeeded. We don't hear from those who committed and believed and yet didn't make it. People don't write (or read) books with titles like "The Seven Habits of Dismal Failures" or "Bad to Worse."

That's why you need effective action. Sure you need commitment, but commitment alone isn't enough, as we are sadly reminded by gamblers who commit and lose their last dollar. What else you need depends on what you want: Cash or partners to start a business, education to get a job, practice to hone a skill, a coach to help you through the rough spots, courage to make the first move. And what else you need depends on what you have now: Your skills, your financial resources, your style, your personal preferences, and so on. (Any plan that relies on my athletic ability would more properly be called "gross self-delusion" rather than "effective action.") Much of *Nice Start* is about action that's right for you.

You might think about that classic question, why are you here. Look all you want for messages, signs, direction, advice, and commandments. Ultimately, though, you are the one who answers that question. That's true even if you think you're being given the answer, because you decide whether to accept the answer. For instance, here's an answer you would presumably reject: In a predestined bureaucratic mistake someone entered your name on a birth certificate, and you were born to prevent the waste of a certificate form, so whatever you do you have already fulfilled your life's purpose. If you reject that answer — which, incidentally, neither you nor I can prove is false — you are demonstrating that you decide the answer.

With the power to decide comes responsibility. Not in the sense of blame or fault; rather, in the sense of ownership. Ownership-responsibility is not something to shirk. It is something to celebrate. If you are free you must be responsible, and if you are responsible you must be free.

Welcome, use, and enjoy your freedom to be yourself.

Good is what the good man does. The good man is the one who does good.
Aristotle (384 BCE–322 BCE)

Gentle

Maxwell feels that he's not good with people. Every awkward encounter seems to validate his assessment. Sooner or later, lo and behold, there Maxwell is, not good with people. Or he's not good with numbers or cooking. Whatever it is, Maxwell has taught himself about himself.

Mildred considers herself good with people. She feels people like her. She feels comfortable with people, which makes them relax with her, and so everyone has a good time and she is good with people. Or maybe she is good with numbers or cooking. Mildred has taught herself about herself.

I'm not suggesting that it's all in our minds and that we can magically become good with people, numbers, or cooking by instructing ourselves in a firm, clear voice. I am suggesting that what we believe about ourselves influences what we do and how well we do it. We humans tend to live up, and to live down, to our expectations and beliefs.

What happens if we think differently about ourselves? That is, not that we come to a different conclusion, but rather that we have a different thought process. What if we think about what we think about ourselves? Let me illustrate.

When I think of myself, I think sometimes of what I see in a mirror. I am five feet nine-or-so inches tall. I am redecorating my hair in grey. I have brown eyes. I have a nice smile.

Other times I think of what I am. Businessman, author, friend, boyfriend, ex-husband, son, brother, nephew, employer, customer, homeowner, taxpayer, middle-aged, American, man.

Sometimes I think of what I am like or what I hear people say about me. Nice guy, smart, good listener, low-key, risk-taker, compassionate, articulate, neat, loving, funny, careful, supportive, organized (really?). I also see parts I don't like: shy, impatient, demanding, uncertain, not-spontaneous, stiff, isolated, perfectionist.

Every now and then I find myself in a quiet, contemplative mood and I open up to what I really believe about myself. No pressure, no fear, no pretense, no nonsense, no judgment, just get real and see where it leads. How might I change my life if I discover and embrace something new about myself? Or not exactly new; just newly recognized or accepted. For instance, it was in a let-the-truth-shine-in moment that I allowed myself to be confident. That's hugely changed what I choose to work on, such as writing *Nice Start*.

In one of those quiet, contemplative moods, I welcomed a few descriptive words about myself. I let them sort themselves out to find which one is closest to what feels like my core. It was a surprise at first, and now I smile every time I think of it.

Explorations

Do whatever you do to enter the mood where interesting, from-the-heart thoughts seem to pop into your head. Inform your mood that you'd like to hear your heart tell you about yourself. Then, listen. (If you hear something negative, then I gently suggest that you are not yet listening to your heart.)

What are 10 positive words or phrases you heard about yourself?

Underline the 3 that seem especially close to who you are.

Circle the one that's at your core.

Knowing that about your core, what will you do differently?

Your Joy

What's something about you that you're eager to share with others?

What's the most beautiful thing you've ever seen?

What's the most beautiful thing you've ever heard?

What's the most beautiful thing you've ever said?

What's the most beautiful thing you've ever done?

Where in your life have you compromised and you're glad you did?

Where in your life have you not compromised and you're glad you didn't?

What would you like to teach?

What would you like to learn?

What are you most proud of?

What's your fondest memory?

What's your favorite place?

What do you collect?

What do you look forward to?

Who looks forward to being with you?

School Today

Little Madison and Makenzy blast into the house. *"We're hoooooome!"*

"How was school today? What did you learn?" The kids eagerly recount their exciting day of geometry, English, physics, history, and more.

Adults are immersed in school-of-life subjects such as relationships, work, dreams, finance, health, etc. However, we rarely do the "what did you learn today?" routine even though we attend our schools every day.

Some challenges have come up in my life-school. Why did I think of them as challenges? I could just as easily have thought of them as problems, puzzles, opportunities, or gifts. The first lesson for me: Notice how I interpret a situation. If I see challenges, I create one set of responses; if I see opportunities, I create different responses.

"You have four oranges, two trash cans, and one box of oil filters." In regular school we're told whether our assignment is for math, home economics, or English. In life-school, we, the students, label the subject. My second lesson was in how to assign the labels. Work? Relationships? Values? The subject I select defines the solutions I consider.

When you read "their exciting day of geometry, English, physics, history, and more," did you see it as tongue-in-cheek humor? That illustrates my third lesson: Whether today's curriculum covers geometry, English, physics, and history, or whether it covers work, relationships, and values, we get to choose whether it's an exciting day.

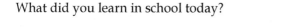

Explorations

What did you learn in school today?

Look at the details of your life today. Where did you see problems, issues, challenges, opportunities, gifts, or something else? Where could you have seen things differently?

Was your day exciting? Will tomorrow be exciting?

The most exciting phrase to hear in science, the one that heralds the most discoveries, is not 'Eureka!' (I found it!) but 'That's funny'.

Isaac Asimov (1920?-1992)

Getting a "D"

I turned in a homework paper soon after I entered Yale. It came back with a lurid, scarlet "D." It was not followed by "arn good work." It was just a D, all by itself.

At first I thought the professor couldn't spell. Surely a D was a mistake. After all, I'd never gotten a D or even a C in high school. D? Impossible! Yet there it was. D.

Though more than 35 years have passed since my D Day, I remember my shock and outrage. "Who does he (the professor) think he is? <pause> Oh. He is a professor at Yale. He is an expert in his field. I am a freshman taking an introductory course in a discipline new to me. Hmmm."

I decided my chances of learning were greater if I listened than if I resisted. I decided learning mattered more to me than looking good (as though I would've looked good if I'd insisted the professor was wrong). Result: I changed my study habits, my grades improved, and I learned.

D's don't come only in school. A speeding ticket; a rebuke from a boss; a money-losing financial decision. D's give us feedback essential for learning and growth. (D's aren't always right and don't always mean we're wrong. A good decision at the wrong time may get a D.) And D's are not fatal.

I've gotten plenty of D's in my life. Even when they hurt (do they have to?), they always mean I'm getting feedback. I've paid the price, and I might as well reap the benefit of learning from that feedback. That part is up to me.

Explorations

List 5 D's you have received.

Which of the D's you've received had the biggest positive impact? Why?
Which of the D's you've received had the biggest negative impact? Why?

List 5 D's you have given intentionally.

Which of the D's you've given had the biggest positive impact? Why?
Which of the D's you've given had the biggest negative impact? Why?

And let's not forget the A's. List some A's you have received and given.

There can be no deep disappointment where there is not deep love.
Martin Luther King, Jr. (1929-1968)

What You Want

We don't always know, or admit, what we want. We have our own self-imposed political correctness. We think it's okay to advocate and desire some things, and not others. We censor ourselves.

You are looking for a new car. You may say you want a safe, sensible, economical car, because you think you should. You may actually want a cool sports car to go zoom-zooming down the road, your hair (if any) whirling attractively in the breeze as admiring throngs admire you.

You are dating. You may say you want a meaningful relationship and that looks don't matter, because you think you should. You may actually want a meaningful relationship with a person who turns your brain to heaving hormonal mush whenever you look at him or her.

You are looking for a job. You may say you want to climb the corporate ladder to great wealth. You may actually want to devote your life to community service. Or vice versa.

One of my teachers said you can have anything you want if you're willing to pay the price. (Everything has a price, which isn't necessarily money.) How much are you willing to pay for zoom-zoom? How much of your brain are you willing to devote to heaving hormonal mush?

The point is not self-indulgence; the point is honesty. If you really, truly want the zoom-zoom car, go for it. If you don't, don't. If you really, truly want the hunk or babe, go for him or her. If you don't, don't.

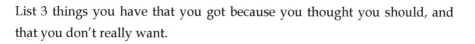

Explorations

List 3 things you have that you got because you thought you should, and that you don't really want.

What would happen if you got rid of those things or stopped getting more things like them?

List 3 things that you think you shouldn't want and that you really do want.

What would happen if you let yourself go get them?

Those who restrain desire,
do so because theirs is weak enough to be restrained.
William Blake (1757-1827)

Do you prefer a stop sign or a traffic light?
(*The Book of Numbers*, R.J. Berman)

Wrong

We are born ready and able to express what we feel, and we don't judge our feelings. We don't worry about being wrong or stupid.

That changes. We grow self-conscious, capable of feeling embarrassment, afraid of being wrong or looking bad. Kids laugh when we give the wrong answer in school. (Why do they laugh and why does their laughter hurt?) We get sweaty and tongue-tied when we ask someone out, or we compensate with swagger and machismo. (It's a wonder anyone ever gets a date.) You should see the horrified looks on people's faces when they hear me say I love public speaking. They look as frightened as I probably look when they say they like to dance.

Do we learn those fears by living in a culture that rewards boldness, competitiveness, and success? Or is it something inherent in being human? I don't know.

Here's what I do know. That "loser" is a terribly dismissive insult. That corporations and governments suffer from groupthink because people don't want to look weak, different, or dim. That experiments show people will say things they know are wrong rather than be the only one to give the right answer. That people do things that they know are wrong because they want to be accepted or because they are told to do so. That people believe things that have been proven wrong. That overconfidence costs lives. That it is imperative for politicians always to be right lest they be accused of flip-flopping. How awful it would be for a politician to say he or she has learned something new!

My point is not that you or I shouldn't care about being wrong. My point is also not that every person falls into the don't-be-wrong trap all the time. My point is simply that in our society it is very important to appear right. We learn that, and we behave accordingly.

Later on, many of us spend time and effort undoing all that, getting to the point where we can say "I'm wrong" or "I don't know." I found that journey difficult at times, and surprisingly liberating. I learned that the pressure I previously felt was self-imposed, and as soon as I stopped judging myself for saying "I'm wrong" or "I don't know," I felt less stress in my life. Oddly enough, I found that my credibility with others went up, not down, when I could admit error or ignorance. That happened because I annoyed fewer people with meaningless arguments and because I didn't make believe I knew something that I didn't.

I don't like these cold, precise, perfect people who, in order not to speak wrong, never speak at all, and in order not to do wrong, never do anything.

Henry Ward Beecher (1813-1887)

I was gratified to be able to answer promptly. I said I don't know.

Mark Twain (1835-1910)

What have I done?

Alec Guinness (1914-2000) as Colonel Nicholson in
"The Bridge on the River Kwai" (1957)

Explorations

Do you think less of people who say they're wrong or they don't know?

Do you think less of yourself when you say you're wrong or don't know? (If you never say those things, your answer is evidently yes, you would think less of yourself.)

Would you vote for someone who says that he or she was wrong or ignorant about something? Would you vote for someone who didn't?

What do you really have to lose by saying you're wrong or you don't know?

Good judgment arguably requires experience. Even if that's true, it doesn't mean that experience always produces good judgment. How do you know when what you have learned is right, not wrong?

No one should be ashamed to admit they are wrong, which is but saying, in other words, that they are wiser today than they were yesterday.

Alexander Pope (1688-1744)

Reasons For

Here's a way I risk my internal reputation for clear thinking. Step 1: I make up my mind. Step 2: I pretend I haven't. Step 3: I look for information that confirms what I pretend I haven't decided. Step 4: It's done! I've compiled such compelling data that my (original) conclusion is (now) inescapable.

That efficient, enjoyable process may not have life-altering consequences. "Honey, we might need a new TV. I just happened to see an ad for the TechnoBlast ZYX321, and it will save us so much energy it'll pay for itself (if we keep it for 42 years). And the beer cooler at the bottom means I won't walk so often to the kitchen, so we'll save by not having to replace the carpeting!"

There's another version of justifying a conclusion that goes deeper, affecting how we think and what we believe. We might sum it up like this: Do you buy books with which you expect to disagree?

Social psychologists write about *confirmation bias*, the tendency of human beings to accept reasons and data that support their beliefs and to dismiss reasons and data that don't. If you believe climate change is fictitious, you will believe people who say it is fictitious, and discount those who say it is real. If you believe climate change is real, you will do the reverse.

Confirmation bias doesn't feel like bias; it feels like truth. Our judgment even shows up in our words: we often say "you're right," not "I agree."

Because confirmation bias is unconscious, it's hard to know when it's happening. Because it's part of being human, it's hard to fight. Because it prevents us from listening, it hurts our ability to make good decisions.

If I like a person or position, I find reasons for supporting him, her, or it. If I don't like a person or position, I find reasons for believing he, she, or it is sadly misinformed. Satisfying, maybe. Fair and effective, not so much.

Confirmation bias is a kind of mental cheerleading in which we look for reasons for what we think. Hooray for the noble arguments from our side, down with the poisonous, dastardly heresy from the other side. Sound like a political campaign? We don't have debates, we have advertisements.

We learn reasons-for thinking in school, in business, and in government, where the objective is to make our case. We win points by accumulating noble arguments for our side. We lose points by saying "on the other hand, our esteemed opposition makes sense when they say…" We may even lose points for esteeming the opposition.

Research shows the antidote to confirmation bias is to look for reasons against. That is, look for reasons why you might be wrong.

Being human (drat), I have overlooked the reasons-against approach at times. For instance, I willfully, consciously ignored warning signs in a budding relationship — well, okay, in more than one — by focusing on the positive and assuming we'd iron things out as we go. It turns out that the warning signs had been worth reading.

Looking for reasons why you might be wrong does not mean you *are* wrong (though none of us is always right). It means only that you'd rather learn you are wrong (if you are) early, before you've committed time or money to a mistake. The worst that can happen is that you learn more and get a reputation for wisdom and open-mindedness.

Explorations

List 5 beliefs, judgments, or decisions that really matter to you.

List 3 *reasons for* you used as you adopted the belief, judgment, or decision.

List 3 possible *reasons against* it.

To be, or not to be

William Shakespeare (1564-1616)

Undeniable Evidence

What would you do differently if you had undeniable evidence that:

You were reincarnated and you chose the life you are now leading?

Someone you love will die within one month?

You will die within one month?

You could save the lives of 100 strangers by giving half of your money?

People like you were happier living in another country?

You'll live 10 years longer if you sleep 1 hour more (or less) per night?

Watching (or not watching) TV significantly reduces your creativity?

You've chosen the wrong career?

There is life on other planets?

One of your cherished beliefs about religion or politics is wrong?

You are happier (or sadder) than most people?

You can do better?

Barking Flowers

On *America's Funniest Home Videos,* an adorable little girl leaned toward a flower. As her nose was about to touch it, a dog (which she couldn't see) barked. She jerked back from the flower, as though *it* had barked. (Maybe it was a dogwood.) She sent it an adorable little frown.

We know flowers don't bark, so we look for other explanations (e.g., a dog). Other times, though, we apparently believe flowers bark. We do that when we unconsciously or uncritically obey *prior hoc, ergo propter hoc.* (Translation: if A precedes B, then A caused B.) It's more than a pompous Latin way to finger the cause of an effect. It's also the recipe for superstition.

Tom drives a new route to a ball game, and he strikes out. Conclusion: Bad route. Next time he won't drive that route, cementing his belief by repeating it to himself. If he gets a hit, he steel-reinforces the cement. "It worked!"

When we believe something, we can cause that very thing. If Tom forgets and drives the bad route to a ball game, he'll be so nervous when he gets to bat (why oh why did I go that way, I should have remembered, I'm going to let my team down and they'll hate me and I'll have to go into exile) that he might as well give up and save the pitcher the trouble of throwing the ball.

The number 13 is a barking flower. We shun it so much, we actually skip the 13th floor in most American hotels. (Does that fool anyone?) I've asked dozens of people in hotel elevators why they think a 13th floor would be so unlucky. Either no one knows or I've asked the wrong people.

Explorations

Look around and see where people behave as though flowers are barking. Quirky habits are a fertile source. For example, the lucky shirt treasured by someone you know (not you or me, of course) even though it's been reduced to a few out-of-style fibers held together by desperate quantum forces.

What are some barking flowers you observed today?

How are you watering and feeding your own barking flowers?

Where does luck come from?

Bonus question: If we're so afraid of 13th floors in hotels, why don't we shun 13 as a row number on airplanes?

It is bad luck to be superstitious.
Andrew W. Mathis (?)

The more I practice, the luckier I get.
Attributed to both Arnold Palmer (1929-) and Gary Player (1936-)

Obvious

How sure are you that you are not overconfident?

I am very sure that you *are* overconfident. Why? Because you're human. Reputedly being human, I am overconfident too, though I don't know how sure of that I should be. The overconfidence part, not the being-human part.

Psychologists have devised ingenious experiments that demonstrate overconfidence. (See Sources.) I've conducted one of those experiments many times in my speeches around the world, and I replicate their results every time in every country. The same experiment showed I'm overconfident too.

Confidence can be charming, attractive, and effective. Overconfidence, not so much. When you and I go into overconfidence mode, we stop listening. Why listen? We already know the answer. *They* should listen to *us* because we *know*. Overconfidence makes us arrogant, even angry. It makes us jump to conclusions. It makes it hard for us to learn. It makes us make mistakes.

I suspect overconfidence when I hear the word *obvious* (even when I say it). "It's obvious they just want more money from me, that's why they're trying to sell me the premium model." "It's obvious he's spreading rumors about me." Maybe they do want more money, maybe he is spreading rumors. And maybe not. I've been shocked enough times when people have told me what I was "obviously" thinking or doing, and I wasn't. They were wrong, and I have been too. I'm pretty sure.

Explorations

List 3 times when you or someone else said something is obvious. Circle the one that seems the most obvious of all.

List as many good reasons as you can — there are some — about why it might not be so obvious after all. You don't have to agree with the reasons.

Marketing and politics contain many messages based on "obvious." List and critique several examples of such messages. They may not use the word "obvious;" instead, they may link a message to a powerful word or image.

So far, which questions in *Nice Start* have had obvious answers?

Can one be taught what he does not already know?

Unknown

There is nothing as deceptive as an obvious fact.

Sir Arthur Conan Doyle (1859-1930)

Yourself

Worth Knowing

This exploration was inspired by my uncle, who created the lists to which I refer below. He gave his permission to be written about as follows.

My uncle's remarkable book, *The Book of Numbers,* contains nearly 900 pages of lists: "The Hundred Greatest Buildings," "Great Composers," "Reading for a Lifetime," and much more. "Some Paintings You Should Know," spanning over 500 pages, is stunning. One could say that these are his "my favorites" lists. Yes, and a bottle of Chateau Petrus is full of grape juice.

His lists fascinate me because they organize and present astounding knowledge of Western humanities. My life would be well-lived if I used his lists as a guidebook. *Go to these places. See these things.*

At another level, his lists fascinate me because they are a recording of a lifetime; that is, they *are* a lifetime, and they are required a lifetime to create. A biography contains the accumulated, interpreted events of a person. His lists contain the accumulated, interpreted knowledge of a person.

Moreover, they contain knowledge worth knowing.

In each of our lives there is an amazing uncle or aunt, an accomplished parent, a well-traveled friend, a favorite teacher, someone whose knowledge is worth knowing. That person may be close at hand, or may not; the teacher is available to the willing student. ("You want a ride, stick out your thumb.") Art, music, architecture, literature, science, philosophy, sculpture, engineering, history, locations, animals… knowledge is there for you.

Explorations

What knowledge is worth knowing?

Where or from whom can you get the knowledge you want?

What knowledge do you have that you could contribute to others?

Who might want that knowledge?

If I have seen further, it is by standing on the shoulders of giants.

Sir Isaac Newton (1643-1727)

So Long, Sandman

Some phrases stick in our heads. Something crushing said in anger. Something beautiful said in love. Something wise said in counsel. Something funny said in jest. Something poignant said in farewell.

Those life phrases are miniature time capsules that may sound different as we and our lives grow. A hurtful remark from childhood might generate good-old-days laughter later on. A perplexing profundity might suddenly make sense. A forceful opinion might be sobering or shocking as our perspectives change. A forgotten compliment might bring a smile, confidence, warmth, or longing.

We use some life phrases to remind ourselves of our core values, especially in times of stress or decision. One I use is, "No one gets up in the morning intending to be a bad person." That thought helps me be compassionate.

Life phrases entertain, intrigue, remind, charm, sadden, thrill, teach, delight. They replay a world of meaning in a few words. Some that affect me:

> "I choose to do this event."
>
> "Life is too short to _____."
>
> "What do you want?"
>
> (derisive, mocking laughter)
>
> "There are no rules."
>
> "Will this matter in a year?"
>
> "So long, Sandman."

Explorations

List 5 of your life phrases.

Why do those phrases stick with you?

What theme do those phrases have in common?

How do those phrases shape your life?

An angel has no memory.

Pygar (John Phillip Law, 1937-) to Barbarella (Jane Fonda, 1937-),
in *Barbarella* (1968)

Music

If you hear a message over and over and over, it seeps into you, especially if you welcome that message into your life. That makes music uniquely persuasive, since we voluntarily listen to songs over and over and over. Most of us can recite lyrics from many songs.

Some songs send negative messages: misery, loneliness, scarcity, anger, hostility. Others are positive: happiness, togetherness, fulfillment, peace, love.

What would happen if you listen for years to songs about unrequited love, being left for someone else, how awful men or women are, and how hard it is to find the right one? What would that do to your attitudes about relationships? I don't know, of course. I also don't know what effect it would have on your attitudes about relationships if you listen for years to songs about dancing together, having fun, and being in love. However, it seems reasonable to me that those songs have *some* kind of effect, in the same way that movies, stories from friends, fairy tales, negative people, positive people, and so on, shape our attitudes.

Music hath charms to soothe the savage breast,
To soften rocks, or bend a knotted oak.
William Congreve (1670-1729)

Only sick music makes money today.
Friedrich Nietzsche (1844-1900)

Explorations

What are your favorite songs? What messages do they send?

Do you like those messages? If not, why do you let them in your life?

Would you want a child — your child — to receive those messages?

What television shows do you watch? What do you read? What's on your walls, your own personal billboards?

Humour is a great vehicle for getting a message across.
If you get too serious, you could die of starch.

Cyndi Lauper (1953-)

My life is my message.

Mohandas Gandhi (1869-1948)

Being Marlon Brando

Marlon Brando died in the summer of 2004 after a remarkable life in which he was called perhaps the greatest American actor. Critics and movie-goers say he "defined" his roles.

What does it mean to "define" a role? To me, it means that he let it all out, he didn't hold back, he committed 100%, he shared his intensity and vision. By the accounts I've read, he lived his life that way, too. Imagine being Marlon Brando, living and acting at that level!

When I was a small child, I was defining my role; I was being Marlon Brando with my own name. I let it all out, I didn't hold back, I committed 100%, I shared my intensity and vision. So did you. You were being Marlon Brando, with your own name. The difference between Marlon Brando and me is that he kept being Marlon Brando. I, on the other hand, gradually became less Marlon Brando. I became cautious, I became careful, I checked before I committed, I asked permission before I shared my intensity and vision.

Some things in my life have helped me get closer to being Marlon Brando. Brushes with death that reminded me to live. Insights in personal-growth seminars that helped me unlock the Marlon Brando inside me. Watching Marlon Brando being Marlon Brando, and being aware of what I admire about his life.

I don't plan to audition for a remake of *The Godfather*, unless they make me an offer I can't refuse. However, thinking "Marlon Brando" helps me be me. Thank you, Marlon Brando, for the gift you gave us.

Explorations

Write about how being Marlon Brando would feel in your life. What would you think, feel, do, or appreciate differently if you were more Marlon Brando?

Others

No one's perfect except you and me, and sometimes I'm not sure about you.

Unknown

The world contains 6,600,000,000 people. Of them, 6,599,999,999 are not you. If you come in direct contact with, say, 30,000 of them during your life, you directly impact 0.00045% of the world. (By "direct contact" I mean more than bumping into nameless people on buses or in movie theatres.) Meeting 0.00045% is roughly like reading one letter in this book.

You have indirect impact on many more people through the friends and family you influence, the actions your employer takes, the taxes you pay, the charities you support, the products and energy you use, the candidates you vote for, and so on. Your impact on any given person in the world may be microscopically tiny. Add up all your big and small impacts, though, and in sum you make a difference in the lives of others. Meanwhile, others near and far make a difference in your life.

Of course the differences we make aren't one-way streets or one-time events. I do something that impacts you. You perceive the impact. You respond. I perceive the impact of your response. I respond. On and on.

People engage in many interactive relationships: wife/husband, parent/child, buyer/seller, politician/voter, country A/country B, and more. People often say, "He or she just doesn't get it." People rarely say, "I'm not communicating it." People often say, "She or he is unreasonable."

People rarely say, "I am unreasonable." People often say, "You started it." People rarely say, "I started it."

Psychologists talk about the "fundamental attribution error." It's what happens inside our heads when we figure *they* did something bad because they are intentionally evil, and if *we* do something bad it is because we were forced to by the situation. In other words, we erroneously attribute intentions. Berfel was aiming for my window with his football; he's always had it in for me. My football hit Berfel's window because my cell phone rang and distracted me; it wasn't my fault.

Sometimes they *are* at fault, at least from our perspective. There are people who want to hurt us. (Let's remember too that there are people we want to hurt.) Those who want to hurt us don't think of themselves as bad; they think of *us* as bad and deserving of being hurt, and they think of themselves as good and righteous. We reverse the characters and say the same thing.

The point is not to make nice with everyone and it's not to say there is never a right or wrong. The point is that we humans often make mistakes in assuming who is at fault, or even that there *is* fault as opposed to accidents. In other words, when we say someone is at fault it always *feels* as though we're right, when in fact sometimes we are right and sometimes we are wrong.

The point is also that it's awfully hard to get someone to back off simply by walloping them, literally or figuratively, while insisting we're right. Would you change your mind because someone walloped you and snarled that you're wrong, evil, and degenerate? Thanks for screaming that I'm a horrible person, I'd love to renounce my whole life and agree with you.

The fundamental attribution error might explain how both sides in a conflict can genuinely believe the other side started it. It might explain why murderous hatreds survive for hundreds of years. *Hundreds of years.* That means wanting to avenge something that someone said happened to your great, great-grandparents, more or less. The pain, the suffering, from relationships based on a *tradition* of hate that we teach our children… Is it all about having the last word or last blood? (They started it!) What will it take for people — them and us — to say "enough"? (Do you respect the person who gets the last word or the person who takes the first step?) How extraordinary, the terrible, terrible things we do to each other.

And how extraordinary, the kind things we do for each other. People spend their lives working for others' benefit. People give their lives for strangers. People devote their lives to knowledge and service. We don't always fall into the fundamental attribution error; sometimes we love and trust. There are acts of kindness that don't make "rational" sense, such as leaving a tip in a restaurant in a far-away place that you know you will never visit again. (Such observations have inspired a fascinating field called behavioral economics.) Cooperation is so important, studies suggest evolution hard-wired it into us.

One of humanity's basic, often-cited relationship guides is the "golden rule": do unto others as you would have others do unto you. What, though, if others don't want done unto them what you want done unto you? You love olives, you lovingly hand me a plate generously filled unto overflowing with them. I don't like olives; really, I don't. I would much rather have a plate filled unto overflowing with anything else, except for beets and a short list of other vastly overrated so-called delicacies. What if, as I read somewhere, we rephrased the golden rule this way: do unto others as they would have you do unto them. In other words, give 'em what they want, not what you want 'em to want.

Sometimes, despite good intentions, we don't give 'em what they want or they don't give us what we want. My first marriage ended in divorce. I find it unsettling that one day I could look at a woman and honestly say that I could not imagine my life without her, and ten years later I could feel otherwise. She is a good woman, I think I am a good man; it wasn't bad faith, bad intentions, or misdeeds by her or me. Yet it just wasn't right, and all our efforts couldn't make it right.

I felt awful about our divorce. Why? After all, we solved our relationship problems, and we solved them honorably, amicably, and correctly. Yet I felt I had failed. I felt I had fallen short of my (and perhaps her) expectations of what a good husband is and does.

My second marriage ended when my wife of eight months told me on the telephone that she was not coming home. I presume that she felt her departure was a suitable solution for whatever problems she perceived, because if she didn't she wouldn't have done it. I don't know where in the world she is. I don't even know why she left. All I know is that that relationship did not go as I'd expected, nor, presumably, did it go as she had expected.

I don't think of my marriages as sad stories. I cherished both and consider myself lucky to have enjoyed them. When I think of them now, I see how they illustrate expectations. I don't mean expectations about who takes out the garbage. I mean expectations about behavior, attitudes, and communication in a relationship. Marital pledges such as fidelity and honesty, if made, are negative in the sense that they are promises of what you or I *won't* do (cheat and lie). What positive expectations can we have of each other?

Others

As I write these words in 2008, the United States is in the midst of its quad-rennial election spasm. Much of what we hear is implicitly about relation-ships and expectations. For instance, what contributions (e.g., taxes) do we expect of each other? What social behaviors do we want to encourage and discourage? For what are we responsible as individuals and for what as a nation? How do we balance responsibility against mercy? How should we interact with other nations? Whom do we trust to make weighty decisions on our behalf?

Speaking of the president of the United States, of course some people influ-ence more people than others. Yet there is no one on earth who is known to everyone on earth.

We have many ways to classify who is "us" and who is "them." Ethnicity. Nationality. Gender. Age. Home town. Religion. Political party. Style of dress. Occupation. Wealth. Language. Size. Hobbies. Intelligence. Athletic-ism. Education. Seniority. And so on. The often-unconscious judgment of whether a person is *us* or *them* makes a difference in how we perceive their motives and trustworthiness. Of course *they* do the same thing, which means we've got a lovely opportunity for a vicious circle. This is how per-verse it can get: Experiments show that when *our* side's ideas are presented as coming from *them*, we reject the ideas. When *their* ideas are presented as coming from *us*, we accept the ideas. (We'll revisit that perversity in They.)

Let's think for a while about what unites us, not what (we think) divides us. We want to get along, we want to accept and be accepted, we want to do what's right, we want to enjoy precious human contact. Understanding oth-ers, and helping others understand us, helps that happen. We spend our lives inside one body and it can be hard to see the world the way 6,599,999,999 others do.

A teacher once told me, "I didn't say it would be easy. I said it would be worth it." To which I add that it doesn't *have* to be not-easy; we don't have to make it difficult. Relax, and enjoy getting to know the rest of us.

No one ever has the last word.

Jack Balkin (1956-)

Roles

Who are you?

If a stranger asks you that question, you may respond by describing your occupation. I am a bank teller. I am a schoolteacher. I am a lawyer. I am unemployed. (Does having no occupation mean I'm not someone?)

Who is that person? If you look at a stranger, you may think about his or her occupation. He is a foreman. She is a manager. He is a pilot. She is a doctor.

We often interact role-to-role, especially with strangers. She is a manager, I am a customer. He is a pilot, I am a passenger. Names are secondary, even irrelevant.

We've all seen people be rude, abrupt, or demanding to others. We even think it's justified. "He's the salesman, he's supposed to know." "She's the flight attendant, it's her job." That's because we see the role, not the person.*

If the salesman were your uncle Albert, if the flight attendant were your neighbor Donna, you'd see the person, not the role.

---

* It can get much worse when we dehumanize others, as Philip Zimbardo shows in *The Lucifer Effect: Understanding How Good People Turn Evil.*

Explorations

List some people, not among your friends or family, with whom you interact regularly. You may not know their names.

Circle one of those people. Write down 3 specific ways you would behave differently with that person if he or she were someone you wanted to make your friend.

Suggestion: Treat them that way. It's free and it'll make them feel good. Bonus: They're not the only one who will feel good.

How do you think your country's government should treat people, including you? Assume everyone in the country will be treated the same way.

Do you think your country's government should treat all people in your country the same way? Why or why not? Would you be willing to see your answer, with your name attached, on television?

There's a man who is my brother / I just don't know his name.
"It's About Time," John Denver (1943-1997)

Doing Good

When you get up in the morning, you probably don't say to yourself, "My goal today is to make really bad decisions. I want to mess things up, offend people, and create havoc and chaos everywhere I go. I will count this day a success if, when my head hits my pillow, I have made the world a worse place."

We're all doing the best we can. We want to do good. We worry about being good enough. We want to be safe, to be admired, to be loved.

We make the best choices we can, depending on what we think is good and on how we perceive our options with what we know at the time. If we think option B is better than option A, we choose option B. That doesn't mean option B is truly good. It merely means that a person who chooses option B believes that option B is the best one available.

What people consider good depends on how they see the world, and based on what people have done there are some awful perceptions of the world out there. Let's leave aside the horrific extremes, though, and get closer to our day-to-day lives.

I had a neighbor who liked wind chimes. They would bing and bong constantly. Unfortunately, I don't like wind chimes, and they drove me crazy. ("Unfortunately" not because it's bad for me to dislike wind chimes; rather, because it put my neighbor and me at odds.) I asked that they come down. My neighbor refused. Tension escalated.

Eventually one of us mentioned why we felt as we did. It turns out that the wind chimes provided a sense of peace and serenity for my neighbor, whereas I felt the wind chimes were a noisy intrusion into my home. Each of us could understand the other's feelings, which helped us see that neither of us was getting up in the morning plotting to annoy the other. It's a lot easier to work things out with a human being than with an ogre. We were able to come up with a mutually agreeable solution that worked well for us.

Polls show Americans are fed up with partisan politics. Both parties profess the purest intentions — the good of the country — yet they pillory the other party. Democrats are unpatriotic because, we're told, they want to negotiate with the enemy. Republicans are unpatriotic, we're told, because they want to export jobs. Is it possible that both Democrats and Republicans are human beings, not ogres? (Maybe with a few exceptions. Just kidding.)

We communicate more deeply, thoughtfully, and compassionately when we see the world through others' eyes and remember we're all doing the best we can. It might give you new perspective to think about why a human being could sincerely see good where you see bad, or how a human being could justify actions that you consider inexcusable. You don't have to agree with their viewpoint to understand it.

Explorations

During a discussion or debate, ask the other person why they believe their position is good. Listen sincerely and don't argue. Restate their position to them until they're satisfied you understand it. You don't have to agree; you just want to understand their position and why they believe it.

As Anna Freud remarked, the toddler who wanders off into some other aisle, feels lost, and screams anxiously for his mother never says "I got lost," but accusingly says "You lost me!" It is a rare mother who agrees that she lost him! She expects her child to stay with her; in her experience it is the child who has lost track of the mother, while in the child's experience it is the mother who has lost track of him. Each view is entirely correct from the perspective of the individual who holds it.

Bruno Bettelheim (1903-1990)

Irrational

My boss is so stupid. She doesn't realize how much money the company wastes.

My husband is driving me nuts. Doesn't he see the kids are out of control?

We might think that the boss and the husband are irrational, incompetent, or careless. However, what about the people — including the boss and the husband — who think they're *not* irrational, incompetent, or careless? How do we decide who's rational? Majority vote? Who gets to vote?

Assume for a moment that the other person is smart and rational, and then ask why a smart, rational person would behave that way. Maybe the boss has other priorities, or she wants not to fire anyone, or she's been given bad information about the amount of waste, or she knows something you don't. Why not ask? Maybe the husband wants not to constrain the rioting kids, or is letting them tire themselves out before bed, or has an agreement with them that says they can run amok at certain times. Why not ask?

I worked on a consulting project with a large, successful company populated by smart, rational people. One of their people, a particularly smart and rational guy, spoke about what motivated his colleagues to perform well. He drew a chart that had common business metrics — profit, growth, and so on — at the top. He then asked "why is that important?" for the metrics. He connected the metrics to other metrics and activities. Why is *that* important, he asked of those. And he kept asking until he got to the bottom line: Profit, growth, and so on, are important because they help me keep my job and provide for my family.

You get what you pay for. If you award bonuses or preserve employment on the basis of, say, sales growth, you'll get sales growth. You may get other good things too, but if sales growth is what you pay for, don't be surprised if people sacrifice the other good things to grow sales.

Of course, it's not only about bonuses or jobs, or even about money. It's also about affection, recognition, self-esteem, status, and so on. If you get rewarded in whatever currency matters to you for doing X and for not doing Y, you're more likely to do X than Y.

We want to get paid (in our preferred currency), so we take action that we think will produce what we get paid for. Perhaps our actions are effective and perhaps not; perhaps we had better options and perhaps not; perhaps we noticed a problem and perhaps not. We are human, after all. The point is that, to us, our actions are not irrational. If we thought we could produce better by doing something else, we'd do something else. When we hear a complaint and we respond with "you don't understand my position," we're saying that you don't understand the links we perceive between our actions, our options, and what we want.

Of course, maybe the boss and the husband really don't know what's going on. A question from you may be just what they need.

Explorations

List 3 events when your friends or family thought you were irrational or careless.

Circle the one they thought was the most irrational and careless. List 3 reasons why they might think so. You don't have to agree with them.

List 3 events when you thought a friend or family member was irrational or careless.

Circle the most-irrational, most-careless one. List 3 reasons why they might think their behavior was sensible. You don't have to agree with them.

Bonus exploration: Talk to him or her about their or your irrational or careless behavior. Share your thinking, and ask about theirs. Remember that it's about understanding. It's not a debate.

> *There is nothing so extravagant and irrational*
> *which some philosophers have not maintained for truth.*
> Jonathan Swift (1667-1745)

Twins and Everyone Else

This essay was written by a friend of mine.

Most of us have known at least one set of identical twins, and some of us have fantasized about being one of such a pair. The set I knew initially were roommates from California in my first year in a college dormitory; they said (or one of them did) that only their mother could tell them apart, that even their father and siblings had difficulty. They spoke in shared sentences, dressed alike, played substitution games with others, seemed to have their exclusive idiolect (or <u>bi</u>alect), never argued or even appeared to disagree, laughed together, ate a bag of potato chips together, drank (although alternately) from the same bottle of beer, held hands, took the same courses when I knew them, studied in the library and laboratory together, slept together, manifestly sought each other's companionship over that of any other. They were seventeen then and I have no idea of what became of them; many decades later I often think about Bill and Will (or Ron and Don, or Larry and Barry).

In the archer's target below, theoretically anyway, Matt and Pat would be — seem? — together at the core, marked 100, or EGO. The rest of us would individually be alone there, a single and singular <u>I</u>. At 99 might be my spouse of seventy-five years, to whom I have told all there is for another to know about me (well, except for this and perhaps *that*, that other thing I would never demonstrate or verbalize to anyone capable of learning or remembering; and Rover, who knows *all* about me, doesn't count), and that's why even said dearly beloved spouse can never be my twin and join me at my 100. I might feel very close indeed to someone, who would then make it into the 90's, less close to another, who would then be in the 80's, and so on. I don't know him or her too well but strongly want to (70's), somewhat less so for that other (60's). I know his, her name (I think), and he, she might know mine (below 0); I might have enjoyed a companionable dinner or two, drive, tennis match, symposium, chat over the fence (10's, perhaps even 20's). I like her (34) but like him just a bit more (36).

Others

Explorations

Mark by initials, an initial, the name(s) of your current love(s), dear friends, friends, cohorts, acquaintances, whatever you would term them, according to their current consociations or relationship to you (of course, from *your* own unique prospect). How close is X, truly? And Y? You might want to distinguish male (♂), female (♀), transgender, and other, younger and older (→ and ←), frequency of meeting (Daily, Weekly, Monthly, about once or twice a Year), rising (↑) or (alas) falling (↓) in your affections, designation (wife, daughter, father, any familial relationship), professional associate, employee, neighbor, friend, companion, drinking buddy, whatever (compose your own symbols); even living (good) or gone (not so good [perhaps, perhaps not]). If you are as honest with yourself as you might find yourself capable, you might be interested to know who is where in your circles relative to others, and at what levels, and the far larger number hovering about the periphery. (Note: You might want to update your chart every six months or so.) (And a further note: Sharing your archer's target with another somewhere or other [or not] on it could be quite hazardous to your consociations; only identical twins could feel safe in that [or so it might seem].)

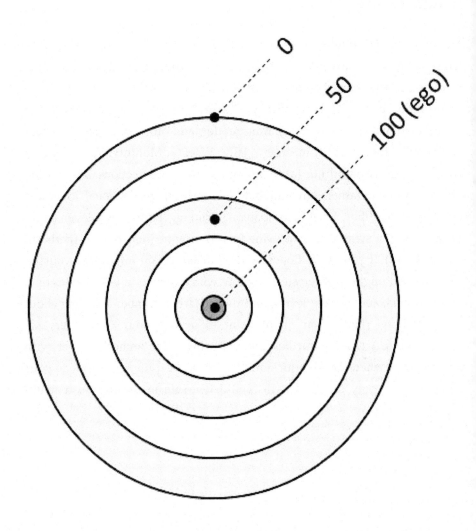

The Battle of the Sexists

Men don't get why women complain about being sex objects. Men think women have it made, being desired and courted, getting what they want with a smile. Women know women will stand by their men; women fear their men will run if they lose their charms or a prettier, younger thing beckons. Women know men don't pursue unattractive women, so they hide their wrinkles.

Women don't get why men complain about being success objects. Women think men have it made, making decisions, being taken seriously, having money. Men know men will rescue a damsel in distress; men fear their women will run if they lose their income or a richer man beckons. Men know women don't respect (let alone rescue) men in distress, so they hide their distress.

It doesn't help when we demonize each other, claim victim status,
and demand that the other make the first move.
It doesn't help to argue about who bears the heavier burden.
(That's a question no one can answer and a debate no one can win.)
Let's recognize that both genders have power,
both genders have vulnerabilities, both genders feel responsibilities,
both genders make sacrifices, and both genders have gripes.
And both genders want to love and be loved.

All I want is someone to love me.

Emily, in *Our Town,* by Thornton Wilder (1897-1975)

Explorations

Write down some unwritten expectations of each gender. "Men/women are supposed to…" You can find them in movies, songs, fairy tales, laws, etc.

What is the expectation of your gender that annoys you the most or puts the biggest burden on you? Does your significant other know you feel that way?

What is the expectation of the other gender that you imagine would be the biggest burden to bear? Why?

What is an expectation of the other gender that your significant other lives with without complaint? Does he or she know you appreciate it?

What is an expectation of your sex that you feel you live with without complaint? Do you feel appreciated by your significant other?

If I give myself, can I ask for you?
"*Short Stories*," Harry Chapin (1942-1981)

I married an archaeologist because the older I grow,
the more he appreciates me.
Agatha Christie (1891-1976)

Promises

I remember the day I first got married. My family came out in droves, and so did my soon-to-be wife's. Our happy friends poured in. The great doors opened and I saw my fiancée in her wedding dress. I was thunderstruck, and if anyone had been foolish enough to look at me instead of her, they would have seen a man, mouth hanging comically open, waiting for his brain to reboot. I could not imagine being with anyone else for the rest of my life, and a few minutes later I said so to the assembly.

Ten years later, we were divorced. Amicably, to be sure, and we are friends. Yet here we are, man and woman, not husband and wife.

After that experience I questioned my confidence in promises, including my own. Perhaps I was innocent or naïve to have that confidence in the first place; then again, it's been a long time since I was a starry-eyed youth. Regardless, I felt I had betrayed her and my word. I felt I had broken a solemn promise I had given in total certainty I could and would keep.

Can I be trusted, by others or by myself? I spoke with honesty when I asked her to marry me, and I spoke with honesty when I asked her for a divorce. Maybe it is (only) my honesty that can be trusted.

Never say never, we say. Should we also say, never say always?

Explorations

What are 3 promises you have made to others and that you have broken?

What do you trust in yourself?

What are 3 promises others have made to you and that they have broken?

What do you trust in others?

It is not the oath that makes us believe the man, but the man the oath.
Aeschylus (ca. 525 BCE-ca. 456 BCE)

The very first law in advertising is to avoid the concrete promise and cultivate the delightfully vague.
Bill Cosby (1937-)

Stand Up

I was in London with my uncle Robert, having a drink in the lobby bar at the Ritz. A very, *very* fancy party was going on around us.

Our waitress, wearing an evening gown, suddenly came to our table and whispered urgently, "Stand up!" We stared at her, puzzled. When we didn't budge, she whispered as forcefully as she could, "*Stand! UP!*" We saw her go as rigid as a Marine at attention. We followed her gaze and saw, not 10 feet from us, Queen Elizabeth stroll by.

We were stunned… and frozen in our seats. After the Queen passed and we regained consciousness, we were mortified that we'd appeared disrespect-ful. Had we understood, had our waitress said "please stand for the Queen," of course we would have stood.

Two days later I addressed a conference in Canada. Half the audience was American, half was Canadian. I told the story and asked who would have stood when told only "Stand up!" Every Canadian said yes. Every American said no. Not right or wrong; simply different cultures.

George Bernard Shaw described England and America as two countries se-parated by a common language. Even when we think we communicate clearly, others may not understand. They're not necessarily intending to be difficult.

By the way, if you talk to Queen Elizabeth, or if you are Queen Elizabeth: our apologies.

Explorations

List 3 episodes when you (or someone else) said something that other people apparently heard differently.

When have you appeared disrespectful to others and you didn't mean it?

When has someone been disrespectful to you and (possibly) didn't mean it?

Living is easy with eyes closed, misunderstanding all you see.
John Lennon (1940-1980), "Strawberry Fields Forever"

Ever since Eve gave Adam the apple,
there has been a misunderstanding between the sexes about gifts.
Nan Robertson (1926-)

Stereotypes

Gorgeous female computer scientist. A figment of an adolescent geek's fevered imagination? A convenient character for the movies?

Some of my friends pointed to a picture of a beautiful woman on the cover of a computer magazine and laughed at the idea that a beautiful woman would even be interested in computers. They were surprised when I revealed that I had dated a real-life woman with a Ph.D. in computer science who was even more beautiful than the model on the magazine.

Some stereotypes make some sense. A jock is probably physically fit, a chess master is probably analytical, a CEO is probably ambitious. Other stereotypes are questionable, yet we're often willing to believe them: the dumb jock, the antisocial chess master, the greedy CEO. Others, of course, are so repugnant that we reject them.

Harvard sponsors an ongoing study that measures subconscious reactions to various topics. For instance, it told me that I have a "strong automatic preference" for classical music over hip-hop music. No big surprise. I was surprised, though, when it showed me that some of my conscious beliefs conflict with my subconscious attitudes (stereotypes), as they do for most people. That's what happened with my friends. They might believe that a gorgeous female computer scientist is theoretically possible even though they, without thinking, laughed at the idea.

Did you?

Explorations

Visit www.implicit.harvard.edu/implicit to participate in the study and learn about yourself. It's free, confidential, and fascinating.

STEREOTYPE: A shoe designed to fit all feet within a particular ethnic or social group. When the shoe actually fits, as it sometimes will, the satisfied salesmen exchange sly winks across the room.

The Cynic's Dictionary, Rick Bayan (1950-)

Life Studies

What do you want students (of any age) to learn that they don't know now?

About happiness

About the arts

About science

About creativity

About tolerance

About leadership

About communication

About different cultures

About citizenship

The direction in which education starts a man
will determine his future life.

Plato (ca. 424 BCE–ca. 348 BCE)

What do you want students (of any age) to learn that they don't know now?

About the environment

About responsibility

About competition

About cooperation

About success

About thinking

About manners

About giving

About receiving

Human history becomes more and more a race
between education and catastrophe.

H.G. Wells (1866-1946)

It is the mark of an educated mind to be able
to entertain a thought without accepting it.

Aristotle (384 BCE–322 BCE)

They

They're a bunch of morons. They're all crooks. It's impossible to reason with them.

"They" are out to get me in some way, to enrich themselves at my expense, to sacrifice me on the altar of their cause. "They" are worse than wrong. They are willfully wrong, they are evil.

Talking about "them" reinforces the bond of "us" between you and me. They are not us. And if you're not for us, you must be for them.

It's safe to talk about "them" when "they" are unnamed. It's still reasonably polite, and we don't sound like fanatics. We let the listener fill in the blank to identify "them."

Who are "they?" Get specific, get honest about who "they" are and why they are such villains. Are they really villains, or do you just need someone to blame for something? Are they doing the best they can (just like you) with the information available to them (just like you)?

To them, you are "they." Which, of course, proves how nasty "they" are, because "they" have the temerity, ignorance, or viciousness to revile you.

It takes courage and a clear head to break that vicious circle.

I'm not whining that we should all just get along. I'm not saying you have to agree with them. I'm not denying the existence of real evil, and I'm not talking about real evil in this exploration. The issue isn't conflict; the issue is vilification.

Here's how much we're against "them." (I'm replacing the names with A and B so that we're not distracted by who "they" are.)

> In one experiment, [social psychologist Lee] Ross took peace proposals created by A negotiators, labeled them as B proposals, and asked A citizens to judge them. 'The A's liked the B proposal attributed to A more than they liked the A proposal attributed to the B's,' he says. 'If your own proposal isn't going to be attractive to you when it comes from the other side, what chance is there that the *other* side's proposal is going to be attractive when it actually comes from the other side?'*

As I write, the 2008 election is in full swing in the USA. The Republicans question the Democrats' patriotism because they believe the Democrats are advocating policies that will endanger the safety of the nation. The Democrats are incensed because they believe the Republicans are saying the Democrats don't love their country. Of course both parties want to ensure safety and both parties love their country. The election-year posturing and vilifying is a far cry from thoughtful debate about how to ensure our safety.

By the way, could you tell whom I consider "them" from my description of the parties' positions? Although I have a strong preference, I think I didn't reveal it. My intention was to focus on the issue, not on "them." If you think I did reveal my preference, that shows how difficult it can be to communicate neutrally.

Let's think more broadly. "They" aren't always people we think are bad; sometimes they're just a separate group. Still, how we think of "them" says a lot about how we think. I run a consulting firm. People ask, "How many

---

* *Mistakes Were Made (but not by* me), Carol Tavris and Elliot Aronson

people work for you?" I answer, "None." I say that because my colleagues don't work *for* me; they don't work to serve me or make me rich. They work for themselves and their families. I say too that I work *with* a number of colleagues. Watching my language about "them" keeps me mindful of my relationship with my colleagues and of the gratitude I feel because they've chosen to work with me.

Another "they" is government. Our complaints about government are the flip side of our hopes and expectations for government. I'm not going to point to the craven promises, partisanship, and pandering of politicians. I'm also not going to sing the praises of the programs and progress, wrought by politicians, that have incalculably enriched our lives. Instead, I'm going to tell the story of my parking ticket.

I left a restaurant, walked to my car, and found a ticket on the windshield. I'd parked in a space reserved for car pools. The sign was right there; I guess I'd been in my own little unobservant world when I parked. I was guilty, no question, no excuse. I felt embarrassed. As I wallowed in remorse (well, let's not get carried away), an irate woman approached me. She'd gotten a ticket too, for the same reason. She didn't seem remorseful or embarrassed. She dramatically expressed her opinion of the injustice that "they" had inflicted on us, and seemed to expect me to commiserate on cue. I said well, we *did* park where we weren't supposed to. She huffed off, perhaps updating her mental records to include me among "them" rather than "us."

The point is not about guilt, remorse, or injustice, and the point is not who was right or wrong. The point is how we view "them."

Explorations

List 3 "they" statements that you or others make. Get specific about who "they" are. List 3 "they" statements you've heard them say about you.

What are they (and you) assuming about you (and them)?

Step back and make believe you're a neutral observer. Express both sides of a conflict using neutral language, as I intended to do with the patriotism / security issue. What did you learn?

Vilify, vilify, some of it will always stick.
P.A. Caron de Beaumarchais (1732-1799)

Who you are speaks so loudly I can't hear what you're saying.
Ralph Waldo Emerson (1803-1882)

In 1929 the wise, far-seeing electors of my native Hereford sent me to Westminster and, two years later, the lousy bastards kicked me out.
Frank Owen (?)

I do not want people to be agreeable,
as it saves me the trouble of liking them.
Jane Austen (1775-1817)

How to Change Someone's Mind

When's the last time someone convinced you to switch sides by pounding you with how right they are and how wrong you are? When's the last time you convinced someone to shift by shouting "I'm right! You're wrong!" louder than they did?

Bludgeoning isn't usually the best way to change someone's mind. If we shout "I'm right!" and back it up with withheld love, withheld paychecks, or rifles, behavior may change; the mind doesn't. Force leads to compliance, not persuasion.

Sometimes we change our minds when we become aware of facts. I changed my diet when I learned more about nutrition. Other times, changing our minds has to do with beliefs. If you believe that all politicians are crooks, debating the success of a particular government program may not change your mind.

When I play a game, I assume that I may win or lose. Why would I play if I don't have an opportunity to win, and why would you play if you don't? Changing minds is the same thing: I have to be open to the possibility that *my* mind may change if I want you to be open to the possibility that yours may change.

Explorations

List 3 times when someone changed his or her mind because of what you said. What worked? (Hint: Avoid the "because I was sooooo right" rationale.)

List 3 times when someone didn't change his or her mind despite your contagious enthusiasm, irrefutable logic, and encyclopedic knowledge. Why didn't it work? (Hint: Avoid the "because he or she is a closed-minded wretch" rationale.)

Reverse the questions above so that they're about you changing or not changing your mind. What worked and what didn't work with you?

Positive, adj. *Mistaken at the top of one's voice.*

The Unabridged Devil's Dictionary, Ambrose Bierce (1842-1914?)

There is no human problem which could not be solved if people would simply do as I advise.

Gore Vidal (1925-)

Smile

I read about an experiment in a credible journal (perhaps *Scientific American,* though I really don't remember). In it, people were randomly assigned to one of two groups. Group A was told to hold a pencil sideways between their teeth. In that position, it's almost impossible not to smile. Group B was told to hold a pencil like a cigar in their lips. In that position, it's almost impossible to smile. (Think of Clint Eastwood in those spaghetti Westerns.)

Both groups, while holding the pencils, were shown a series of cartoons. The group holding the pencil sideways, who were virtually forced to smile, rated the cartoons funnier than those whose pencil position prevented them from smiling. Same cartoons, different reactions.

The implication: Our bodies influence our moods and our perceptions of the world. So, smile! The world will look better to you. Plus, it's what scientists call a positive feedback loop: your smiles make others feel better, so they smile back at you, which makes *you* feel better, so you smile more.

Smile when you talk on your phone. Smile when you sit home alone. Smile when you watch your TV. Smile when you're thinking of me.

Smile at people today. Family, friends, acquaintances, strangers; just smile. See how you feel, see how people react. We all admire and want to be around people who seem to be having a good time, so what have you got to lose? The worst that can happen is that people will think you're happy. And, based on that experiment, they could be right.

Explorations

Notice your smiles today, especially if they're new smiles (that is, you smiled at times when "normally" you wouldn't). When did you smile? How did you feel when you smiled? How did others react when you smiled?

Bonus exploration: do some other smile-like stuff today. Laugh a little more. Stand a little straighter. Wear favorite clothes or shoes. You can do those things, and others, any time and any place.

Every time you smile at someone, it is an action of love,
a gift to that person, a beautiful thing.

Mother Teresa (1910-1997)

One who smiles rather than rages is always the stronger

Japanese proverb

Begin your day by smiling at yourself in the mirror.

Kitty Carlisle (?) (1910-2007)

Laugh

A woman and I got a bit tipsy together. We were close, and we were having a grand time. I observed that she was more than a little talkative, and, just for fun, I said that I'd bet she couldn't stop talking for 30 seconds. She's competitive as well as talkative, and she said, "Okay. When do we start?" I said, "Now." She said, "Okay," and she was mystified when I burst out laughing.

Why am I sharing that story? First, that woman is no longer in my life, and it's a way for me to remember a good time we had together and to express my appreciation for her. Second, because laughing is good, and there's always time to laugh.

When do we start? Now.

You grow up the day you have your first real laugh at yourself.
Ethel Barrymore (1879-1959)

Laughter is the shortest distance between two people.
Victor Borge (1909-2000)

You will look back on the times you laughed and you will cry.
You will look back on the times you cried and you will laugh.
Unknown

Explorations

Laugh.*

* If you need help to complete this exploration:

Watch a funny movie. (Hint: "Duck Soup" is a funny movie. "The Exorcist" is not a funny movie.)

Call up a funny friend. Say, "make me laugh." Beg if you must.

Read a joke.

Tell a joke.

Make up a joke.

Assume that somewhere, someone is telling a joke.

Go ahead, just *laugh! Something* is funny, even if it's just a person holding a book who starts laughing because the book said to.

Acts of Kindness

Write down an unsolicited, unexpected act of kindness you can do for each of the following people, without expecting or accepting anything in return. It doesn't matter how big or small the act of kindness is.

A relative

A friend

A former friend

A co-worker

A neighbor

A stranger

Someone helping you (a waiter, postal worker, salesperson, etc.)

Someone who works for the government

Someone much older or younger than you

Someone much richer or poorer than you

Someone in another city

Someone in another country

Explorations

Look back at the acts of kindness you identified on the previous page. Circle 3 or more of them to do today. Do them today.

How did it feel to do them?

For extra fun, make giving acts of kindness a family activity.

For variety, do them anonymously.

For a great habit, do one a day for a month, a year, or a lifetime.

What acts of kindness have people done for you recently?

People talk about the nobility of sacrifice. Is it necessary for the giver of kindness to suffer in some way for his or her act to be good and kind? Put another way, can Bill Gates' acts of kindness be as good and kind as a poor person's? For that matter, can a poor person's acts of kindness be as good and kind as Bill Gates'?

> *Three things in human life are important. The first is to be kind.*
> *The second is to be kind. The third is to be kind.*
>
> Henry James (1843-1916)

Others

Acts of kindness do not have expiration dates. That point came home to me when I received a phone call from a woman whose name I didn't recognize. She told me that *30 years ago* I'd loaned a little money to her and her friend when they were street musicians in Boston. (They were strangers to me at the time and we've had no contact since then.) I hadn't given the money a second thought. She did. Many years and thousands of miles later, she tracked me down. She offered to repay me and she thanked me for the kindness I'd shown her and her friend. She told me of the difference I'd made in her life and that my generosity was even more impactful than the money.

It was a tiny action on my part, nothing special, less than a drop in the ocean of kindnesses that people perform every day. Her call, though, was special. *That's* what my teachers have meant by an attitude of gratitude, and that's what my newest teacher has demonstrated.

To that woman, as she reads this book: thank you. You made a difference in *my* life. I will remember.

And as for you, dear reader: what acts of kindness have others done for you, perhaps long ago, that you would like to acknowledge?

Hmmm. If you'll excuse me, there's someone I'm going to contact…

The only people with whom you should try to get even
are those who have helped you.

John E. Southard (?)

Thankful

I am thankful for the road workers who labor at night so I'm not inconvenienced, and who create the nice, smooth roads that make driving a pleasure.

I am thankful for the people at the car dealership who wash my car when I bring it in for service.

I am thankful for the letter carrier who delivers impossibly misaddressed letters to me.

I am thankful for the newspaper delivery person whose strong arm and accurate aim mean I don't have to walk far from my door on rainy days.

I am thankful for the person who rings up my groceries with a real smile.

I am thankful for the friend who makes sure I know about a TV show that I might like.

I am thankful for flight attendants who work hard to make sure I am happy and comfortable.

I am thankful for people who prepare for emergencies that we all hope will never come.

I am thankful for the technical-support experts who politely tell me the eight-number DNS server identifier my computer needs to connect to the Internet using TCP/IPv4, whatever that is.

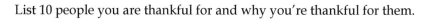

Explorations

List 10 people you are thankful for and why you're thankful for them.

Circle those you haven't ever thanked or haven't thanked in a long time.

Tell them you're thankful for them.

It's okay to include yourself in the list.

*As we express our gratitude, we must never forget that
the highest appreciation is not to utter words, but to live by them.*

John F. Kennedy (1917-1963)

*Appreciation can make a day, even change a life.
Your willingness to put it into words is all that is necessary.*

Margaret Cousins (1905?-1996)

I am thankful for laughter, except when milk comes out of my nose.

Woody Allen (1935-)

Perspectives

Taken as a whole the world may be round,
but in my neighborhood it is unquestionably flat.

Mark Twain? (1835-1910)

Today you woke up in the body you lived in yesterday. What if you didn't? What if today you woke up with the same mind, the same memories, the same self, at a different address? Perhaps you'd be inside the body of a Peruvian shepherd, whose previous occupant has made other arrangements. Perhaps you'd be inside the body of a housemaid on Park Avenue, an actor in Hollywood, an infant in Iceland, a nurse in Namibia, a supermodel in Italy, a soldier in Iraq, a poacher deep in a jungle, a sweat-shop worker, a bus driver, or a subsistence farmer. Perhaps you'd be inside the body of someone who belongs to a group you despise. Perhaps you'd be inside a rich body, a dying body, an athlete's body, a shackled body.

It would be *you* inside that body, yet everyone around *you* would see the body. They would understand and judge *you* based on what they saw. Why would they do otherwise? They don't see *you*. They see your body, what it's wearing, and what it's doing.

You see the bodies around your body. Who's inside? Maybe someone just like you, maybe someone sworn to destroy people just like you. A philanthropist, a couch potato. Someone good and decent, someone depraved and malevolent, someone downtrodden and fearful. How do you know?

The next day, you get a new address. And the next, and the next. You're king for a day, beggar for a day, talk-show host for a day, new widow for a day. You never know where or who you'll wake up tomorrow. All you know is that *you* will be inside.

How would such an existence change the way you think the world ought to work? Would it change your attitudes about, say, war and peace? How about your attitudes concerning tolerance and charity? Would you speak differently? Would you listen differently? Would you judge differently?

Having lifetime, nontransferable leases on our bodies, it is a challenge for us to see the world through others' eyes. Yet it is the ability to imagine another's perspective that gives us insight and compassion.

I participated in a social exercise with 30 other people. Each of us was dealt a card from a deck of playing cards. We held our cards on our foreheads so everyone could see our cards while no one could see his or her own. Some of us were lordly kings and queens. Some of us were lowly deuces.

The exercise was for us to wander around the room, talking briefly to as many people as we could, with one special instruction: the further "above" the other people you thought you were, the more you were supposed to talk down to them, and the further "below" the other people you thought you were, the more you would be deferential and meek. (You had to figure out your own rank based on how others treated you, keeping in mind that they didn't know their own rank.) So, if you figured you were royalty — jack, queen, king — and you saw me holding a three on my forehead, you would treat me with disdain and I would infer that I'd better find a way to please you. If you thought the situation were reversed, you'd offer to shine my shoes, fetch my coffee, do my homework, whatever you thought would put you in my good graces.

It was fun, in an awkward kind of way, and it was awkward, in a fun kind of way. Everyone knew it was a game, and everyone knew everyone else knew it was a game, yet still it was uncomfortable to treat (and be treated by) other human beings as superiors or inferiors. It was illuminating to realize that people have different life experiences and thus are used to different positions on that dominance spectrum. Even if one's forehead card closely matched one's station in real life, it could feel painful, frustrating, humiliating, or guilty to lay bare something so deep and private and so intimately connected to who we are.

Early in 2008 National Public Radio broadcast an interview with a former thief, a man who used to break into houses. The interviewer asked if anyone had ever stolen from him. He said yes, someone had recently stolen his video camera. He said, with pain in his voice, that he doesn't care about the camera, he just wants the tape that was inside the camera because it holds his last conversation with his dying father. The interviewer asked him, "When you were a thief, did you ever think that you might be taking precious memories from someone else?" There was a long pause, and then he said softly, "Oh. I never thought of that."

Perspectives mean thinking about that, about seeing things differently. Seeing through another's eyes. Seeing how today's actions affect the future. Seeing with analysis, seeing with emotions. Seeing tradeoffs. Seeing uncertainty. Seeing individually, locally, nationally, globally.

Perspectives can be culture-bound and therefore hard to see. *The Wall Street Journal* reported that in 2007 YouTube was temporarily blocked in Thailand because it contained a video insulting to the king, in which a pair of feet appeared above the king's head. In the USA that image would be puzzling. In Thailand, though, feet are considered the most offensive part of the body.

Perspectives can start with the same information and end in opposite positions. As I write these words, the United States Supreme Court is reviewing a law banning handguns in Washington, D.C.* Everyone agrees that handguns are often used in the city's murders. Yet some conclude from that information that guns ought to be banned, and others conclude from the same information that we need guns for self-protection.

Perspectives affect us unconsciously. In an experiment some moviegoers were asked "how long was the movie;" others, "how short was the movie." The people asked the first question answered, on average, 130 minutes. Those asked the second question answered 100 minutes.†

Another experiment "asked student football fans from Princeton and Dartmouth to view a short film of a football game between the two schools. Although both sides watched the same film, each side thought the opposing team played less fairly and engaged in more aggressive and unsportsmanlike conduct. The researchers observed that the two groups of students 'saw a different game.'"‡

Perspectives affect our judgment: how do I know what happened, how do I know that *this* is good and *that* is bad? Perspectives affect our sense of right and wrong.

We started this section with *you* in a different body each day. What if you took on new perspectives in other ways? If you like gratification now, what

---

* Update: the Court struck down the law.

† *The Psychology of Judgment and Decision Making,* Scott Plous

‡ *Judgment in Managerial Decision Making,* Max H. Bazerman

would be different in your life if you waited for later? If you save for tomorrow, what would be different if you spent today? If you think about which politician is best for you, what could happen if you thought about which is best for your country or the world? If you assume you're right, what if you assumed that someone else could be right? If you assume only one of you can be right, what if you assumed both of you have valid points?

Suspend disbelief for a few pages. Entertain viewpoints you may not like. Ask yourself why other people believe different things with as much sincerity as you feel for what you believe. Ask yourself what if. Ask yourself why not. You can always go back to what you think now.

Our loyalties must transcend our race, our tribe, our class, and our nation, and this means we must develop a world perspective.

Martin Luther King, Jr. (1929-1968)

How inappropriate to call this planet Earth, when clearly it is Ocean.

Sir Arthur C. Clarke (1917-2008)

It is said an Eastern monarch once charged his wise men to invent him a sentence to be ever in view, and which should be true and appropriate in all times and situations. They presented him the words: "And this, too, shall pass away."

Abraham Lincoln (1809-1865)

Man Loses in Casino!

Now there's a headline you'll never see. It's hardly newsworthy; after all, the probabilities and statistics are not friendly to the gambler, and even the gambler knows it. If you need confirmation, look at the sumptuous buildings in which Las Vegas casinos live. Where did the money for the buildings come from?

The point here is not to send you to or keep you from Las Vegas. The point is to be conscious of how we lose perspective about chance, and how we misinterpret the world as a result.

We see headlines about unusual events *because* they are unusual. We see all about airplane crashes; we see little about car crashes unless they involve some morbid novelty. We hear about children getting hurt on their way home from school; we hear nothing about children making it home safely. We read about the freakishly lucky MegaLottery winner; we read nothing about the legions of lottery losers. And let's not even talk about the movies, which are all in good statistically impossible fun.

What about the other side? Why don't the media report more images and stories of kindness and love? Maybe it's because they are common, not rare.

In real life we see people caring for others all the time. Parents helping their children; friends supporting friends; shopkeepers greeting patrons; letter carriers saying hello as they deliver the mail; soldiers, police officers, and firefighters risking their lives for strangers; teachers pouring their hearts into their lessons; volunteers for charitable and humanitarian causes; artists creating beauty; and on, and on, and on. Not so newsworthy unless there's something curiously heroic, lucky, or sacrificial about it.

According to the Centers for Disease Control (CDC), each year approximately 50,000 violent deaths occur in the USA.* More people die from the seasonal flu: 56,247 in 2006.† The American Cancer Society estimates 565,650 people will die from cancer in 2008‡, amounting to about 23% of deaths in America.

It's ironic: Unusual events look common, attainable, or feasible because we see them in the media all the time. Common events are the silent background, and so we yearn for the good old days when they appeared common (perhaps because the unusual events were less noisy).§ And so we believe that improbable good things will happen to us, we fear the improbable bad things that won't happen to us, and we mourn the perceived loss of our shared humanity.

---

* www.cdc.gov/ncipc/profiles/nvdrs/default.htm. "Violent deaths" include homicide and suicide. You can find the exact definition at www.cdc.-gov/ncipc/profiles/nvdrs/faqs.htm.

† www.cidrap.umn.edu/cidrap/content/influenza/general/news/jun12-08deaths-br.html

‡ www.cancer.org/downloads/stt/CFF2008Table_pg4.pdf

§ The media coverage of negative events has risen much faster than the actual occurrence of those negative events, according to the thought-provoking, must-read book *The Culture of Fear* by Barry Glassner.

Explorations

How hard is it to hit a lottery or a game with 1-in-1,000 odds? To illustrate, take a piece of paper and draw a square such that the square takes up 1/1000 of the paper. How big is the square? (Answer below.)

Imagine you're playing poker and you are dealt a royal flush in clubs. You are pleased. Next hand, you are dealt total uselessness. Which hand is more unlikely? Assume a fair deck of cards and a fair dealer. (Answer below.)

The square on the paper. Assuming you use letter-size paper (8.5" x 11"), you would draw a square that is 0.31" (a little over ¼") on each side. Try it.

The poker hands. The two hands are equally likely. A royal flush in clubs is 5 specific cards. The 5 specific useless cards are exactly as unlikely to arrive. So, one way or another, you will receive an extraordinarily unlikely set of cards every time cards are dealt to you. The royal flush looks more unlikely because of the importance we give it and because we pay no attention to the useless cards after we have cursed them. That's why we think there "must be a reason" when important-looking things happen. Our days are full of equally improbable things to which we pay no attention.

Incidentally, the odds of being dealt a royal flush in any suit are 1 in 649,740. If you drew a square on the paper proportional to those odds, it would be 0.012" on each side, about the size of a dot made with a sharp pencil.

For a little extra perspective, Google "powers of ten" and take a tour through the biggest and smallest things in the known universe.

What Do You See?

I was in a hotel lobby while on a business trip. A boy of 7 or 8 walked by, obviously searching. I asked him what he was looking for. He asked me where he could find a restroom.

It was close by and I pointed to the door. The door said MEN. He walked to it and stood in front of it. He stared at the word and I heard him slowly read it out loud: "Boys." He knew how to read, and he understood what he read (he knew it wasn't a place for females). Yet his brain translated what his eyes saw, according to his view of the world.

Our brains edit our eyes. We see details on a first viewing that, after repetition, we filter out of our consciousness. We ignore movie marquees unless we're shopping for a movie, in which case we pay attention. We don't see mailboxes until we need to mail a letter. We don't even see things in our own homes that our brains have categorized as part of the background. It's probably a handy thing; otherwise, we'd always feel the sense of being overwhelmed that we experience when we travel to a new place.

You've probably experienced looking at a familiar place with "fresh" eyes. That's a great way to stay engaged in life. It's the visual equivalent of stopping to smell the roses, and you can do it any time, any place.

Explorations

Practice seeing the world differently as you walk down the street. How different would it look if you were:

A 5-year-old

An 85-year-old

A miscreant

A police officer

A homeless person

A rich person

A city planner

A cab driver

An anthropologist

A person of another race

A life-long resident

A tourist

Someone moving to the area

A newspaper reporter

An investor

A politician

Your mother

Your father

You, 10 years ago

You, 10 years from now

Bonus explorations:

Carry a camera and record what the world would look like through those others' eyes. Crouch down for the 5-year-old. Blur the focus for the 85-year-old. Think of different photo titles for the homeless person and the rich person photographing a fancy store: "We reserve the right to refuse service," and "My favorite store!"

Carry a camera and record what the world looks like to you. Have friends record what the world looks like to them. Compare photos.

Do any of these bonus explorations in a location new to you.

Stories

I saw the personal bible of a woman who'd been married for many years. She wrote inscriptions from time to time about her feelings. After over 50 years of marriage, she wrote, "We made it!"

Those words both please and trouble me. I feel pleased because "We made it!" sounds joyful: she and her husband lived together for many years, which seemed to make her happy. I feel troubled because "We made it!" could mean that she stuck it out despite misgivings or discontent. Either way, of course, it's a story I'm making up. I don't know the truth. If I say I know, all I'm really saying is that I believe my story.

Ambiguity is fun in movies, theater, poetry, literature, paintings, and so on. Drawing one's own conclusions is entertaining and stimulating. At other times, ambiguity can get in the way. Whether I interpret that woman's words as joy or discontent affects whether I interpret that woman's life as an inspiration or a warning.

She's no longer here for me to talk to, so I'll never know what she meant. What I can do is think about her words. Why do I think she might have been joyful, and why do I think she might have been persistent? What was her life like? What lessons can I learn? How can her words be (presumably) clear to her and ambiguous to me?

Recognizing ambiguity keeps me from making up stories. At other times, though, perhaps there is ambiguity that I don't see. That's when I make up stories and not know that's what I'm doing.

Explorations

Read a newspaper article. How do you decide whether the statements you read are announcements, confessions, interpretations, or something else?

Notice the words reporters, friends, colleagues, politicians, etc., use. What do you observe? What's real and what's story-telling?

Look for stories with your significant other (and your children, if you have any) while watching or reading the news. You may hear stories and others may tell stories. Compare your notes.

All media exist to invest our lives with
artificial perceptions and arbitrary values.
Marshall McLuhan (1911-1980)

As important as it is to recognize ... meaning when it is there,
it is equally important not to extract meaning when it is not there.
Leonard Mlodinow (1954-)

The damage doesn't seem so bad from out here.
C3PO (a long time ago, far, far away), *Star Wars* (1977)

Great Truths

No one could tell me anything when I was 20. Fortunately, it wasn't necessary, because I already knew it all. People who were 40 wanted to tell me their great truths. I didn't want to listen. I didn't *have* to listen.

When I hit 40 I wanted to tell 20-year-olds the great truths I'd learned. Oddly, they didn't want to listen.

So I turned to the 60-year-olds, who, 20 years previously, had wanted to share their great truths with me. I said, "Okay, I'm ready to listen now." Either they'd forgotten what they wanted to say or they remembered I didn't want to listen last time.

These days, I hear others' great truths by reading and listening, I speak my great truths by writing, and I seek great truths by observing with my mind as open as I can make it. I have found that suspending my judgment is immensely helpful in my quest to learn. For instance, rather than thinking "they are wrong to do [whatever]," I think, "I wonder why they think it's right to do [whatever]."

One of my great truths is that great truths do not include "should." Perhaps great dreams do. That, though, is another story.

When I was fourteen, my father was so ignorant
I could hardly stand to have him around. When I got to be twenty-one,
I was astonished at how much he had learned in seven years.

Mark Twain (1835-1910)

Explorations

A great truth might be as simple as "be kind." It might be as practical as "look both ways." It might be as generous as "give the best to the other person." It might be as fatalistic as "there's no future in life." It might be as positive as "remember your smiles, forget your tears." It might be as cooperative as "help others and they will help you." It's whatever you would tell someone who's asked you for advice about life.

Write down a dozen of your great truths.

Share your list with great-truths lists from your friends.

Bonus exploration: Save a copy of your list. Open it in 5 or 10 or 25 years.

All truths are easy to understand once they are discovered;
the point is to discover them.

Galileo Galilei (1564-1642)

To know the road ahead, ask those coming back.

Chinese proverb

Believing

Two men asked a rabbi to help resolve their dispute. The first stated his case. "You are right," said the rabbi. The second stated his case. "You are right," said the rabbi. The puzzled men said, "Rabbi, we can't both be right!" The rabbi responded, "You are right."

We have facts: the earth orbits the sun. (Or, as *Skeptic* magazine put it, "A polio vaccine works even if you don't believe in it.") Facts have been proven true. If they are proven not to be true, we stop calling them facts. We have hypotheses, which are ideas that we can test to see if they are true. And we have beliefs. Beliefs are neither facts nor hypotheses. People hold beliefs whose truth is not testable. People even hold beliefs proven factually false.

Rather than ask only "What should we believe?," we may ask, "How should we choose what to believe?" For instance, you may choose to believe:

What experts believe	What the majority believes	What scientists prove
What your parents believe	The opposite of what your parents believe	What someone wrote in a book long ago
What persecuted geniuses believe	What your significant other believes	What you hear on a TV or radio show
What you figure out for yourself	What you get from idealism or fear	What you're taught by tradition
What authoritative people believe	What smart people believe	What famous people believe

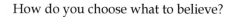

Explorations

How do you choose what to believe?

Do you believe everything you believed 5, 10, or 20 years ago? What made you change your mind (if you did)? Is it wrong to change beliefs?

Think of something you really, truly believe. If there were undeniable evidence that your belief was wrong, would you abandon that belief?

The fact that a believer is happier than a skeptic is no more to the point than the fact than a drunken man is happier than a sober one.

George Bernard Shaw (1856-1950)

Facts do not cease because they are ignored.

Aldous Huxley (1894-1963)

Those are my principles, and if you don't like them...well, I have others.

Julius (Groucho) Marx (1890-1977)

At one time educated people believed that the sun orbited the earth. They believed that bloodletting would cure disease. They believed people would never fly. They believed... well, pick your favorite discredited belief. Remarkably, it often isn't enough simply to use science and evidence to demonstrate that a belief is true or false. We have Holocaust deniers. We have people who believe a person is guilty of a crime despite incontrovertible evidence to the contrary.

What makes individuals — you, for instance — change their beliefs?

What makes societies change their beliefs?

What's something others consider a fact that you consider a belief?

What's something you consider a fact that others consider a belief?

God said it. I believe it. That settles it.
Bumper sticker (seen in Cambridge, Massachusetts)

Every man has a right to be wrong in his opinions.
But no man has a right to be wrong in his facts.
Bernard M. Baruch (1870-1965)

If the teachings of your religion conflict with science, how do you choose what to believe? If you do not believe in any religion, how would you like those who do believe to handle a conflict between religion and science?

What do you *really* believe?

We find it easy to be atheists about other people's religions.

Unknown (similar to Richard Dawkins, 1941-, and Sam Harris, 1967-)

No amount of experimentation can ever prove me right;
a single experiment can prove me wrong.

Albert Einstein (1879-1955)

I try not to think with my gut.
Really, it's okay to reserve judgment until the evidence is in.

Carl Sagan (1934-1996)

Conscience

This essay was written by my dear, courageous friend Adrian Cruz, US Army Reserve, Vietnam Era Veteran 1967-1971. Thank you, Adrian.

As I write on Veteran's Day, I think back 30 years to when a bright-eyed, rather naïve young man actually volunteered to serve his country in time of war.

It would be easy for me now to boast about how brave and patriotic I was, and how much I deserve your well-wishes and praise, on this most somber and sacred day of mourning for fallen comrades. The truth is, I am not a Vietnam Era Veteran because of valor, patriotism, or other high ideal on my part. I joined because I was more scared of the consequences of not serving and evading the draft, than I was of taking my chances under arms.

Many looked in disdain at the thousands of young men who chose not to serve, who burned their draft cards, who went into exile in Canada or Sweden knowing they could not return home. Some chose to call them cowards. However, in the reflection that only comes after decades of introspection and soul searching, I believe their actions actually took more courage than mine. Some lived a life of shame and remorse, wondering which young man on the Vietnam Veteran's Memorial Wall died in their place or if they could look into the eyes of those of us who came home. I, on the other hand, live with my own shame and remorse, wondering if I could have done more to prevent the deaths of some of the men on the Wall.

It all sums up to the fact that nobody won. Nobody was right. Nobody was wrong. We all simply followed our conscience.

Explorations

What's the most difficult decision you've had to make, the one that was more a matter of conscience than any other?

What decisions have others made, based on their consciences, with which you disagreed at the time? (You may still disagree, or you may not.)

Where do you see others (or yourself) insisting that decades-old decisions were indisputably right or wrong? *Were* they (or you) indisputably right or wrong?

> *Labor to keep alive in your breast*
> *that little spark of celestial fire called conscience.*
> George Washington (1732-1799)

Flip It Around

Everyone knows drugs, smoking, and unsafe sex can kill.

It's easy to say that people shouldn't do drugs, shouldn't start smoking, and shouldn't have unsafe sex. The fact is, though, that people choose to do those things, even when they know the risks.

Why do people make choices that don't make sense? It can be illuminating to flip the question around. Why do people think it *does* make sense to make those choices? They are *choices*. Those people are, in effect, saying that they see value in those choices. If they didn't see value in those choices, and if they believed they had other options, they would make different choices. They are good choices for *their* reasons, and we might have no idea what those reasons are. Unless we ask.

A person might get high to relieve boredom or unhappiness. A person might smoke to lose weight or be a rebel. A person might consent to unsafe sex to show love or buy affection. To you or me, those reasons may be dreadfully wrong. To those who make those choices, apparently those reasons are compellingly right.

Explorations

List 5 choices you've seen others make that you find hard to understand.

Circle the one you find hardest to understand. Why might they find that choice attractive?

List 5 choices you've made that others find hard to understand.

Circle the one others find hardest to understand. Why is that choice attractive to you?

Bonus exploration: Talk to someone who's made a choice you don't understand or who doesn't understand a choice you've made. Whoever made the choice presents his or her reasons; the other person listens. The objective is not to debate right or wrong, and it is not to get the listener to agree with the choice. The objective is simply to understand another human being.

There's small choice in rotten apples.
William Shakespeare (1564-1616)

Prisons

According to *The Wall Street Journal* (September 6, 2001), "the number of people behind bars in the U.S. has nearly quadrupled in the past 20 years — to about two million people." We locked up an additional half-million people over the next five years: as of 2006, the number was more than 2½ million.* The cost in 2007 was nearly $50 billion to the states and another $5 billion to the federal government.† We have the highest number and percentage of incarcerated residents of any country in the world. Is that success?

You might say yes. Fewer criminals on streets means fewer crimes. People in prison mean that the system is working and that law-abiding citizens can expect protection and justice. The big numbers deter would-be crooks.

You might say no. Too many people feel they have no better option than crime. More prisoners means more years people spend locked up. More criminals means we failed to prevent crime, meaning more victims of crime.

About 1 of every 100 adult Americans is living behind bars right now. That is a fact. Whether that fact is good or bad is a judgment that depends on how you define success. Put aside notions of vengeance, retribution, debts to society, and law. In your opinion, is it a success? If not, what would be a success?

---

* http://en.wikipedia.org/wiki/Prison

† http://www.washingtonpost.com/wp-dyn/content/story/2008/02/28/-ST2008022803016.html

Explorations

Think about 5 contentious issues in your country: pollution, corruption, crime, violence, health care, taxes, anything that people often argue about. What would be success, in your opinion, on those issues?

Circle the one where, in your opinion, your country's actions are least effective in achieving success.

Think about the issue you circled. What would be 3 specific actions your country could take that would move it closer to success as you define it?

Think about the same issue you circled. What are 3 reasons why others in your country sincerely believe your country's actions are successful or moving it toward success?

What is a country supposed to do and be?

To make us love our country, our country ought to be lovely.
Edmund Burke (1729-1797)

Senator

I do not mean to express agreement or disagreement with a political party or policy. Former Senator Smith gave me permission to include this essay.

I met in Washington, D.C., with Congressional staffers interested in a project one of my companies was working on. My colleagues and I were invited to a reception in the Capitol honoring the passage of legislation sponsored by Senator Gordon Smith of Oregon. The legislation (which was unrelated to our work) authorized money for programs to help prevent suicide.

Senator Smith came in, smiling and shaking hands as I would expect a politician to do. I was introduced to him. I felt fascinated by the process and people, I felt awed by the setting, and yet I felt a show-me cynicism.

The Senator and his wife proceeded to deliver a moving, informal five-minute talk about the legislation. They didn't talk about politics. They spoke about the pain of losing their son to suicide and about their hope that the legislation could help keep others from the same fate. They spoke gently and from their hearts. They graciously and modestly thanked the many people who helped bring their idea to legislative reality.

This, I thought to myself, is what a senator can sound like when the TV cameras are off, when he or she is trying to make a difference in the world.

I spent a few moments with Senator Smith after his speech. I thanked him and told him that he'd helped restore some of my faith and idealistic hope in what people go to Washington to do.

Explorations

What do you believe motivates human beings to enter the world of politics? It doesn't have to be just one thing.

Write down 6 good things politicians have done.

If you find it difficult to identify 6 good things politicians have done, answer this question instead: Why do people become cynical? Suggestion: Think about your experiences and attitudes, rather than blaming "them" and how they "cause" your cynicism.

Bonus exploration: Write to an elected official, preferably one who represents you, and say, suggest, or request something positive.

Bad politicians are sent to Washington by good people who don't vote.
William E. Simon (1927-2000)

When will our consciences grow so tender
that we will act to prevent human misery rather than avenge it?
Eleanor Roosevelt (1884-1962)

Progress

People sometimes question whether we have made real progress. Sure, we have new technologies. What about the social side, though? What about racism, sexism, ageism, and all the other isms that plague us?

Think about what's considered right and normal today. Contrast that to what was considered right and normal not so long ago. In the USA:

100 years ago, most people worked in agriculture. Few do today.

90 years ago, women couldn't vote. That's unthinkable today.

55 years ago, laws in some states separated blacks and whites in schools, buses, and rest rooms. In 2008 a black man was elected president.

65 years ago major European nations were slaughtering each other, less than 30 years after the previous time they slaughtered each other. Today, war among them is virtually inconceivable.

Less than 20 years ago apartheid was peacefully dismantled in South Africa.

And on and on.

We still need to make lots of progress. We have made lots of progress.

Explorations

List 5 common practices, habits, words, or customs that you think most of us will soon consider outdated, inconceivable, or unacceptable.

List 5 common practices, habits, words, or customs that you think will persist even though you think they have already become outdated or useless.

Does progress take too long? How fast should we make progress? How fast *must* we make progress?

In your opinion, who inhibits progress? In others' opinions, how do you inhibit progress?

What should each person — for instance, you — do or contribute so that we can make progress? In other words, how much is enough?

Never discourage anyone… who continually makes progress,
no matter how slow.

Plato (ca. 424 BCE–ca. 348 BCE)

Charisma

*"Those who make peaceful revolution impossible
will make violent revolution inevitable."*

What if I told you that quotation is by Karl Marx?

What if I told you that quotation is by Mohandas Gandhi?

What if I told you that quotation is by Adolf Hitler?

What if I told you that quotation is by Martin Luther King?

What if I told you that quotation is by Mother Teresa?

What if I told you that quotation is by Thomas Jefferson?

What if I told you that quotation is by Oprah Winfrey?

What if I told you that quotation is by Rush Limbaugh?

What if I told you that quotation is by Jessica Simpson?

What if I told you that quotation is by Bart Simpson?

What if I told you I made up that quotation?

Notice how your feelings about the quotation changed as I attributed it to
different people. Who actually spoke those words? See the next page.

The person who said the words I quoted on the previous page is John F. Kennedy. Notice how your feelings change yet again.

The words in the quotation didn't change as I successively attributed them to people great, small, and fictitious on the previous page. Even so, if you're like, oh, pretty much everyone, your comfort with the quotation shifted with each potential attribution. Based on my experience using that quotation in conferences and workshops, my guess is that you felt uneasy about it until you knew who said it.

Why? Perhaps because of cognitive dissonance, a term psychologists use for something that doesn't fit our self-image. You (and I) wouldn't want to say we like a quotation only to find it was said by someone we despise.

We humans work hard to preserve our sense of being right and good. For instance, some prosecutors remain convinced that people are guilty even after they've been definitively proven innocent.* The idea that they locked up an innocent person, sometimes for many years, is unbearable.

Often we know who said something before we know what he or she said. (For instance, we listen to them say it.) We filter, and sometimes unconsciously twist, the words according to how we feel about the speaker. Just think about how you listen to political candidates.

The medium is the message.
Marshall McLuhan (1911-1980)

---

* See *Mistakes Were Made (but not by me)*, by Carol Tavris and Elliot Aronson.

Explorations

List 5 of your favorite quotations. How would your feelings about those quotations change if they were said by someone you don't like?

Just for fun, identify who said these words. Answers are on the next page.

Don't join the book burners. Don't think you're going to conceal faults by concealing evidence that they never existed. Don't be afraid to go in your library and read every book.

Common sense is the collection of prejudices acquired by age eighteen.

Courage is being scared to death - but saddling up anyway.

The weak can never forgive. Forgiveness is the attribute of the strong.

They that can give up essential liberty to obtain a little temporary safety deserve neither liberty nor safety.

Quotation answers

Don't join the book burners. Don't think you're going to conceal faults by concealing evidence that they never existed. Don't be afraid to go in your library and read every book.

Dwight D. Eisenhower (1890-1969)

Common sense is the collection of prejudices acquired by age eighteen.

Albert Einstein (1879-1955)

Courage is being scared to death - but saddling up anyway.

John Wayne (1907-1979)

The weak can never forgive. Forgiveness is the attribute of the strong.

Mohandas Gandhi (1869-1948)

They that can give up essential liberty to obtain a little temporary safety deserve neither liberty nor safety.

Benjamin Franklin (1706-1790)

Numbers

A new stent for abdominal aortal aneurysms is implanted in some patients. Other patients with the same malady receive invasive surgery. There's little difference in recovery rates.* Does that mean the stent didn't help?

On average, men get paid more than women. Does that mean there is pay discrimination?

The stent was given to sicker patients because they were less able to withstand surgery. To know whether the stent helped, we have to adjust for the sickness of the patients who received each treatment. I don't know that answer.

Men work longer hours and in more dangerous (therefore better-paying) jobs. (Men held 54% of jobs in the USA in 2006, and suffered 92% of job-related deaths.†) To know if there is pay discrimination, we have to adjust for experience, hours worked, previous training, job hazards, and more. I don't know that answer either.

We all want good, accurate information that can help us make better decisions. Unfortunately, simple data rarely answer complex questions.

Illiteracy hurts. So does innumeracy. An innumerate person is at risk for making bad life decisions. It's not about mathematics; it's about thinking. Check out *Innumeracy*, a terrific book by John Allen Paulos.

---

* *The Wall Street Journal*, June 13, 2003.

† Bureau of Labor Statistics, www.bls.gov/iif/oshwc/cfoi/cfch0005.pdf.

Listen to the ways people use numbers. For instance, many "surveys" simply invite people to express their opinions, which means that the results can easily be swayed if one side is more likely to see or participate in the survey. As of this writing, CNN.com does exactly that, with their "quick votes." They acknowledge, in small grey print, that "This is not a scientific poll." USAtoday.com has a "quick question" that does not acknowledge the utter meaningless of their "votes." Call-in polls are similarly content-free.

Here's a simplistic use of numbers. Decades ago, General Motors sold as many as half the cars purchased in the USA. In mid-2008 it sold less than 20%.* The cars it produced decades ago are not as dependable as the cars it sells today. Therefore, to increase its sales, GM ought to reduce the dependability of the cars it sells. Right? Of course not.† We might just as well say that GM ought to get the Internet banned, because its sales were higher when there was no Internet. Yet that is exactly the reasoning people use when we oversimplify the complex differences between *then* and *now* to a single contemporaneous factor, say, the growth of China or the demise of Fred Astaire.

One of the toughest numerical questions is the value of a human life. It feels virtuous (why?) to say no one can put a value on human life, and yet we do it all the time. We do it when we decide how much money to devote to medical care for the uninsured or destitute. We do it when we set budgets for police and fire departments, when we spend to control pollution, when we regulate airline safety, when we buy insurance, when we decide how much to give to charity. We do it when we set speed limits on highways. Want to

---

* *The Wall Street Journal,* June 24, 2008.

† Actually, it's not as ridiculous as it may sound at first. Perhaps GM's focus on dependability led them to neglect design, economy, or fun.

cut traffic deaths to zero? Set the speed limit to 5 miles per hour. Don't want to do that? (Neither do I.) You and I are saying that we would rather move fast than have 42,642 Americans make it all the way through 2006.* Or 2,923 Canadians in 2005, about 17,500 Mexicans in 2000, nearly 1,200,000 earthlings in 2002.†

A twist on the cost of life is the cost of death. One could calculate how much the USA has spent to kill each al Qaeda terrorist, each Iraqi insurgent, and each Taliban operative. Even though the exact numbers are contentious, it's pretty clear that we've spent millions to kill each one. Would it be more cost-effective (not to mention less bloody) to buy them off?

Sometimes we look at only one side of an equation. The costs of reducing climate change will be borne in the relatively short term and those costs are relatively apparent. The benefits of reducing climate change — or the costs of not reducing climate change — are harder to quantify. Then again (and this too is part of numeracy), we rarely need precision to make decisions. If the cost of unchecked climate change is (I am making up these numbers) about $70 trillion and 100 million lives in the 21st century, do we really need to know whether it's $69,520,499,121,765 or $71,003,989,243,525? Do we really need to know the names and addresses of those 100 million people?

---

* www.iihs.org/research/fatality_facts_2006/statebystate.html

† Canada: http://www.tc.gc.ca/mediaroom/releases/nat/2007/07h017e.-htm. Mexico: http://www.ingentaconnect.com/content/tandf/icsp/2003/-00000010/F0020001/art00008. World-wide: http://www.pubmedcentral.-nih.gov/articlerender.fcgi?artid=1247497.

Sometimes we think numbers speak for themselves. They don't. What we hear is our interpretations. Take this example. On July 2, 2008, the Wall Street Journal reported on page one:

> The U.S. leads the world in rates of cocaine and marijuana use despite strict drug laws, a WHO [World Health Organization] study said.

Does that mean cocaine and marijuana use is high in spite of the laws; that is, use would be even higher if it weren't for the laws? Or does it mean the laws are ineffective or counterproductive? (Notice that it doesn't matter how precise the numbers are.) Even though "high use with strict laws" may generate emotion — outrage, disappointment, frustration, anxiety — it is ambiguous and not enough for us to draw a fact-based conclusion.

When it comes to drawing conclusions and making decisions, our next question after seeing that brief report should concern why, not what. In other words, is there any information that tells us *why* the USA has that combination of high cocaine and marijuana use and strict laws. We need to know that before we can proceed to *what* we should do. (Well, of course we can proceed to what to do without further information; we just shouldn't pretend that the resulting decisions have anything to do with facts.)

We make decisions about stents, discrimination, quality, life, death, and drugs. In part our decisions are value judgments; for instance, how many traffic deaths we're willing to trade for speed and convenience. Numbers don't make value judgments. Rather, a clear view of the numbers helps us see the consequences, good and bad, of our value judgments.

Explorations

Observe the numbers around you, especially when they are presented by people with points of view to promote. Ask questions about them (the numbers, not the people; well, maybe the people too). For instance, ask the simple question, how do you know? For another instance, take the cost of a national program and divide it by the number of taxpayers.

How should your nation set priorities for spending and taxing? What role should numbers play in setting those priorities?

Experiment and play. For instance, say you have $1,000 that you invest in the stock market. The stock market goes down by 10%, and then it goes up by 10%. How much money do you have now?*

> *USA Today has come out with a new survey — apparently, three out of every four people make up 75% of the population.*
>
> David Letterman (1947-)

---

* Many people answer $1,000, reasoning that the 10% loss and gain cancel out. That's not correct. $1,000 minus 10% equals $900. $900 plus 10% equals $990. What happens if you gain 10% and then lose 10%?

What We Know that Ain't So

Imagine the shock when Nicolaus Copernicus demonstrated that the earth revolves around the sun. People were imprisoned or burned at the stake for believing what he discovered.

In modern times, we are accustomed to breathtaking advances in science. It didn't particularly bother us, emotionally, that the sound "barrier" could be broken. We have come to accept the quantum-mechanics conundrum that Schrödinger's cat can be both dead and alive, if for no other reason than it makes modern electronics work. We welcome stunning technological innovations into our lives even when they challenge what we always knew.

What would happen to our world view if the pyramids in Egypt weren't built by slaves? There is evidence to that effect.* Re-interpreting ancient events could very well cause great controversy and consternation even though it could have no conceivable direct effect on our lives today.

Who is responsible for the quotation, "The trouble with people is not that they don't know but that they know so much that ain't so"? I knew Will Rogers said it. I checked anyway. I found that line (with minor variations) attributed to Josh Billings, Mark Twain, and Will Rogers. Billings' writings predate the others'.

---

* "Who Built the Pyramids?" Jonathan Shaw, *Harvard* magazine, July-August 2003.

Explorations

Which of the following statements comes closest to your view?

Ideas come and go. The eternal truths are what's real.

We should re-examine our thinking as new discoveries come to light.

New ideas are tests of faith.

_____ *(fill in your own)*

List 3 historical events or scientific observations on which your religion, world view, or belief system is based.

Circle the one that makes you feel the most emotionally involved, committed, or disturbed. If you saw undeniable evidence that the historical event or scientific observation you circled were wrong, what would you do or think?

There is no squabbling so violent as that between people who accepted an idea yesterday and those who will accept the same idea tomorrow.
Christopher Morley (1890-1957)

Ignorance is never better than knowledge.
Enrico Fermi (1901-1954)

They Have

They have red lights. They have movies. They have BMWs, Toyotas, and Fords. They have ads for milk starring cartoon cows. They have beer. They have children. They have gas stations. They have parking lots. They have traffic jams. They have police. They have jobs. They have political parties. They have coffee. They have art. They have graves. They have music. They have birds. They have signs. They have homes. They have stores. They have places of worship. They have hopes. They have disappointments. They have love. They have dreams.

They could be just about anyone. They could be in the next house, the next country, the next continent. I've been to over 130 cities on 6 continents, and I have personally verified that they do have all those things there, whoever they are and wherever there is.

They have thoughts and assumptions about us, just as we have thoughts and assumptions about them. Sometimes they're right and sometimes they're wrong. Sometimes we're right and sometimes we're wrong, too.

They may speak a different language, or the same language with a hard-to-understand accent. (I used to live in Boston. I've heard hard-to-understand accents.) They may drive on the other side of the street. They may eat strange foods. Deep down, though, they have exactly what we have: the experience of being human and the desire to live a good life.

Explorations

Pick a city or country other than where you live.

List 3 ways in which the people there are different from you.

List 3 ways in which the people there are similar to you.

List 3 places you'd like to visit.

Circle the place you'd most like to visit.

Start planning your visit.

For those who have seen the Earth from space, and for the hundreds and perhaps thousands more who will, the experience most certainly changes your perspective. The things that we share in our world are far more valuable than those which divide us.

Donald Williams (1942-)

That's Life

Life is tough. Do it to them before they do it to you. An eye for an eye. It's a matter of luck. It's all about who you know. The little guy never gets ahead.

Life is beautiful. There is endless opportunity. People everywhere are basically good. What you put out comes back to you. Go for it, you can do it.

Someone clever (alas, not me) said, "The truth, in my opinion, is my opinion." What's your opinion? Is life easy, is it hard, is it preordained, is it up to you?

I climbed a telephone pole as part of a seminar, with ropes attached to the harness I was wearing. As part of the exercise, I had to let go of the pole (hence the harness and ropes). Since I am afraid of heights, that exercise was excruciating for me. Later, a seminar instructor talked to a group of 30 people who, like me, had "done the pole." He asked what the pole was. Some said, "The pole was hard." Some said, "The pole was easy." Some said, "The pole was exciting." And so on.

He listened to us all, then said simply, "It was a pole." Excruciating, hard, easy, exciting; it was a pole. The rest is what we make of it.

What's life for you? That's life.

Explorations

Write down 3 statements that express your opinion about "that's life." Where did they come from?

How do your opinions about life create your life?

If you were to change your opinions about "that's life," what would you change to?

How we spend our days is, of course, how we spend our lives.

Annie Dillard (1945-)

The opposite of love is not hate, it's indifference.
The opposite of art is not ugliness, it's indifference.
The opposite of faith is not heresy, it's indifference.
And the opposite of life is not death, it's indifference.

Elie Wiesel (1928-)

If my doctor told me I had only six minutes to live,
I wouldn't brood. I'd type a little faster.

Isaac Asimov (1920?-1992), author and editor of more than 500 books

Dreams

Far better it is to dare mighty things, to win glorious triumphs, even though checkered by failure... than to rank with those poor spirits who neither enjoy much nor suffer much, because they live in a gray twilight that knows not victory nor defeat.

Theodore Roosevelt (1858-1919)

Don't you dare close your eyes.

"A Whole New World," Aladdin, 1992
Alan Menken (music, 1949-), Tim Rice (lyrics, 1944-)

Dreams are hopes, aspirations, goals, and fantasies (plus, of course, stories while we sleep). I hope I'll win the lottery. I aspire to be a best-selling author. My goal is to accomplish all the items on my list (see Time's Up). My fantasy is... sorry, I'm not going to tell you unless you're in it. If you want to volunteer... oops, I digress. Never mind.

Dreams are big and small. They are short-term and long-term. They involve ourselves, they involve others, they involve everyone. We are driven to achieve them, we move forward in fits and starts, we fight them, we fear them, we deny them, we love them, we hold them at our core. When we lose our dreams, we exist without living.

All actions begin as thoughts, though not all thoughts produce action. Dreams are thoughts. Sometimes we take action to make dreams come true. Sometimes we don't.

Action without thought is like driving without steering. Look how fast I'm going! It's as though I'm excited by a magnificent opera sung in a language I don't understand, even though I have no idea whether the singers saved civilization as we know it or whether the winsome young maidens will merely merrily marry the handsome young princes.

Thought without action is wishing, hoping, planning, waiting. When I'm ready, boy oh boy will you see something great! I found the perfect suit, made a reservation at the perfect restaurant, ordered the perfect flowers, picked the perfect wine, and pretty soon I'll ask a woman to join me.

If you've only been thinking, it can be scary to move your feet. If you've only been acting, it can be scary to open your eyes.

I find that I vacillate in what I want, which I find disconcerting. Some days I dream about quiet times with the woman I love, enjoying peace and serenity. Life seems simple and happy then, and my only wish is that she and I enjoy good health together and that neither of us has to suffer the loss of the other. Other days I dream about becoming a respected writer, perhaps even admired. I would regret departing this earth with these words trapped inside me. Some days I dream about luxury and travel to places I haven't visited. Some days I dream about making a difference in many lives, through my copious wisdom (which I will begin accumulating any day now) and/or my copious fortune (ditto).

I learn about my dreams in part by watching myself and seeing what I *don't* do. For instance, members of my college and business-school classes have become big-league professors, CEOs of giant companies, and officials at the highest levels of government. I admire and congratulate them for their accomplishments. And I notice that I have not followed similar paths. (We will graciously pass over the uncomfortable question of whether I've got what it takes to make it at those levels.) That's because my dreams are different. Not better or worse; different. Accepting "different" without thinking "worse" is difficult for me sometimes.

Nice Start is one of my dreams. I started thinking about writing a cool book in March 2001 at a seminar. The specific inspiration came a little later, as you saw in the Introduction.

As I'm writing this sentence I've been working on this book for five years. (And that sentence is not the last to be written.) Why is it taking so long for me to translate my thoughts into action? I could blame writer's block and other plagues. I could blame competing commitments. I could blame the amount of work required. When they hear the stories of my struggles my friends nod with sympathy and express encouragement, tinged with sorrow at my painful-yet-stoically-heroic yearning to bring my noble dream to life.

Let me be honest. My excuses are nonsense. They're not why it's taken me so long. It's taken me so long because I've been afraid. My business publications are intellectual and expose little of my ego. With *Nice Start* I feel personally vulnerable. To go forward with a book like this takes a certain willingness to be naked in public (which, for the record, is not my fantasy).

Why do it if I'm so afraid? The simple explanation: because it's my dream. It's hard work, to be sure, and it's also joyful work. I fancy that it makes my experiences, and my reflections on those experiences, worthwhile. It's one of the few things in my life I've felt I have to do. Not "have to" in the sense of obligation. Rather, in the sense of passion and purpose.

In my experience the right questions can generate forward thrust. For instance, not many years ago I was working on an analysis for a client, and I was waffling on my recommendations. One of my colleagues finally got exasperated with me and asked, "If you're not the expert, who is?" Humility is one thing. Paralysis self-induced by false modesty is quite another. That question changed me almost as much as "nice start" did.

The ask-good-questions approach that we began so many pages ago reaches its culmination in this section. No insipid "you go, human!" cheerleading here; the objective is not action for action's sake. Nor is the objective thinking for thinking's sake. The objective is to remember Hillel (page 1) and get real. Who are you? What do you want? When do you want it? If you're not ready now, when will you be? If you don't take action, who will? They're the questions only you can answer, the dreams only you can dream, the actions only you can take, all for the life only you can live.

I don't know anyone who has no dreams, though I know some who take no action to achieve their dreams. I hope that you make your dreams come true, and that you always have more dreams.

Can you even dare to look or beat to think of me: this loathsome gargoyle,
who burns in hell, but secretly yearns for heaven, secretly... secretly...
"The Phantom of the Opera," 1987
Sir Andrew Lloyd Webber (music, 1948-), Charles Hart (lyrics, 1961-)

Got a dream, boy, got a song? Paint your wagon, and come along!
"Paint Your Wagon," 1951
Frederick Lowe (music, 1901-1988), Alan J. Lerner (lyrics, 1918-1986)

I think we dream so we don't have to be apart so long.
If we're in each other's dreams, we can be together all the time.
Hobbes, of Calvin and Hobbes, written by Bill Watterson (1958-)

The Briefcase

I took a cab in New York City. I asked the driver, "How's your day going?" He responded, with some aggravation, that he was still looking for his briefcase. I asked him about it. Here's the story he told me.

"I heard about a cab driver in New York whose fare left a briefcase in the car. The driver opened the briefcase and found half a million dollars in cash in it. That's the briefcase I'm looking for. I want my briefcase."

He didn't know the other cab driver. He believed it was quite possible that someone would leave such a sum behind and not look for it afterward. He was adamant that there was another fully stocked briefcase out there, ready to show up in his cab, and he wanted it.

He said that the episode he described happened 20 years ago.

He had been waiting for his briefcase for 20 years.

To think of him — and he was not a young man — spending so many years so intently focused on something that's not going to happen made me sad. How could he not see? Why would he not see? Tragic.

And I started to wonder, where in my life am I waiting for *my* briefcase? Am I waiting for it, looking for it, or creating it? Is someone waiting for me to give him or her a briefcase?

Explorations

What's in your briefcase?

Who's going to give it to you?

Do not spoil what you have by desiring what you have not; but remember that what you now have was once among the things only hoped for.
Epicurus (341 BCE–270 BCE)

I hope that while so many people are out smelling the flowers, someone is taking the time to plant some.
Herbert Rappaport (1913-1999?)

Dreams

Huntington Hartford

On May 20, 2008, a man named Huntington Hartford died. His death made page one of that day's Wall Street Journal:

> _"Died: Huntington Hartford, 97, A&P supermarket heir_
> _who depleted a fortune chasing his dreams, in the Bahamas."_

The New York Times said:*

> _"Huntington Hartford, who inherited a fortune from the A. & P. grocery business_
> _and lost most of it chasing his dreams as an entrepreneur, arts patron and man of_
> _leisure, died Monday at his home in Lyford Cay in the Bahamas. He was 97."_

"Depleted" a fortune… "lost" most of it… "chasing" his dreams. The Times said, "He inherited an estimated $90 million and lost an estimated $80 million of it." Doing the math… he wasn't exactly destitute, with $10 million left.

Certainly Mr. Hartford was lucky to have had enough money to do as he wished. Was he a failure, though, as "depleted," "lost," and "chasing" suggest? Why didn't the Journal and the Times congratulate him posthumously for "spending" his fortune "living" his dreams?

---

* www.nytimes.com/2008/05/20/arts/design/20hartford.html.

Explorations

Would Huntington Hartford's life have been better if he had not "lost" so much money? If so, why is it bad to "lose" money?

Is it "better to have loved and lost than never to have loved at all"?

"If at first you don't succeed, try, try again." Or is it better to give up and do something else?

How would you recommend that your friends and loved ones live their lives? Do you use the same recommendation for your life?

There is no comparison between that which is lost
by not succeeding and that lost by not trying.
Sir Francis Bacon (1561-1626)

To most Americans the worst errors are financial
and in that respect I have been Horatio Alger in reverse.
Huntington Hartford (1911-2008)

One Wish

Imagine that you can cause any wish to come true. There are just four conditions. First, you get only one wish. Second, your wish must be unambiguous. ("Give everyone what they want" doesn't qualify. For how long? Who is "everyone"? What if someone wants someone else not to have what they want?) Third, it must promote the common good. Fourth, you don't get preferential treatment. Whatever you get, everyone gets.

Cause all nuclear weapons to disappear immediately and permanently. Make everyone immortal. Remove pollution from the air, sea, and land. Whatever you say, so shall it be.

Think about what happens next. What happens after nukes are gone, we live forever, or the earth is green? Would it help to give everyone a billion dollars? The ensuing inflation will quickly devour what initially looked like wealth.

Watch out for assumptions. "Everything would be great if only..." Ask yourself why everything would be so great if only.

Your wish may be for something controversial, and it might even cause suffering. Just remember the third condition, that it promote the common good. Will your wish *really* help?

Your one wish would be your legacy. It is the best thing you can conceive of doing to help the world.

Explorations

What is your wish, the one thing that you think will make the biggest positive difference for the world? Why is that your wish?

Are there any "losers" if your wish comes true? ("Losing" is from their perspective, not yours.)

What is the single biggest problem facing the world?

Why hasn't it been solved? If it were easy to solve, presumably it would have been solved. Does everyone agree it's a problem? Does anyone benefit from the problem's persistence? Is it connected to another, deeper problem?

Unfortunately, not even the awesome powers bestowed upon you by *Nice Start* can make your wish come true. You can, though. What's one thing you can do to move your one wish closer to reality?

> *If you would beseech a blessing upon yourself, beware! lest without intent you invoke a curse upon a neighbor at the same time.*
> Mark Twain (1835-1910), "The War Prayer"

What's the *Problem?*

First-year marketing class at the Harvard Business School. I'm sitting in an amphitheater-style classroom with 83 other students. We are smart, aggressive, competitive, and well-prepared. We know that half our grade depends on class participation. We've each spent hours dissecting a 30-page case study of a real business situation for this class (and hours preparing cases for 2 more classes that day). The class lasts an hour and 20 minutes. There's no way all of us can speak. Gladiatorial combat in a capitalist Coliseum.

The class is half over. We have, as usual, twisted ourselves into an educational, analytical, managerial muddle. Professor Corey, a dignified gentleman who has seen the frenzy before, steps forward and quietly asks (as he always does): "What's the problem?" The effect (as it always is) is like hitting a brick wall.

Oh. We're quoting statistics, we're arguing passionately, we're making decisions, and we haven't even identified the problem we want to solve.

Since that class, it has amazed me how often debates are solely about debating. I've found in my life as a manager that asking "what's the problem?" helps people (including me) get clear and constructive. I've found in my life as a human being that the same question, asked of myself, helps me get clear and constructive when I face a challenge. I've used it to make some of my toughest decisions. Best of all, the more difficult the challenge, the better the question works.

If there's no solution to the problem you identify — where you are is intolerable and getting somewhere else is impossible — perhaps it's not the right problem. Solve a different one.

For instance, when I was working too hard, I was unhappy, I wasn't doing a good job, and business was suffering. As long as I framed the problem as "How can I work harder?" or "How can I adjust to this life?," I kept producing the same sad results. I finally asked a different question: "What work do I want to do, and can I get someone else to do what I don't enjoy?" Eureka! A whole new set of better solutions opened up, and they worked.

If your happiness depends on what someone else does,
I guess you do have a problem.

Richard Bach (1936-)

The way we see the problem is the problem.

Steven R. Covey (1932-)

The best years of your life are the ones in which you decide your problems
are your own. You do not blame them on your mother, the ecology, or the
president. You realize that you control your own destiny.

Albert Ellis (1913-2007)

Explorations

List 3 challenges you feel you confront over and over, without real resolution. Circle one, perhaps the one that's the most vexing.

What's the problem? What do you want? (You may bounce between those questions before your answers feel comfortable.)

Given the problem and what you want, what's a solution?

If you had that, would it solve the problem without creating worse problems? If yes, great! Go do it. If no, go back to the what's-the-problem step.

Bonus exploration: Use this process with another person to solve a problem.

Extra bonus: Solve a problem together that you're having with each other.

They always say time changes things,
but you actually have to change them yourself.
Andy Warhol (1928-1987)

Working

Pick up a device small enough to fit in your pocket, press a few buttons, and you can talk to anyone in the world who has a similar device.

Put a silver disc inside a machine and fill your home with music performed by great (or at least famous) artists.

Step aboard an aluminum tube and, a few hours later, go for a stroll on a different continent. In the meantime, watch a movie or look down at clouds.

Feel cold? Feel hot? Press a button or turn a dial to change the climate. Feel ill? Stand in front of a machine and let someone look inside you. Feel curious? Type a few words, then click "search."

What we take for granted today would be viewed as magic by our parents' parents' parents. Most of the people reading this book are inconceivably rich by the standards of most people living today and everyone living a hundred years ago. Why, then, don't we relax and enjoy it? I'm not saying we should, nor am I saying that we shouldn't. I'm simply noticing that many of us don't. Myself included. If I re-arranged my life, I could live modestly — though still at a level beyond the vast majority of people who have ever lived — without working again. Yet it is a beautiful summer day and I am indoors working on *Nice Start*. I work, and strive, and want even more. Why?

> *We desire, we pursue, we obtain, we are satiated;*
> *we desire something else and begin a new pursuit.*
> Samuel Johnson (1709-1784)

Explorations

List 3 reasons why you work to get more or get ahead.

What are the reasons behind those reasons?

Imagine that your work could be something that feels like playing to you. What would that work/play be?

What work I have done I have done because it has been play. If it had been work I shouldn't have done it. Who was it who said, "Blessed is the man who has found his work"? Whoever it was he had the right idea in his mind. Mark you, he says his work--not somebody else's work. The work that is really a man's own work is play and not work at all.

Mark Twain (1835-1910)

I long to accomplish great and noble tasks, but it is my chief duty to accomplish humble tasks as though they were great and noble. The world is moved along, not only by the mighty shoves of its heroes, but also by the aggregate of the tiny pushes of each honest worker.

Helen Keller (1880-1968)

I know that if I have heaven / There is nothing to desire. / Rain and river, a world of wonder / May be paradise to me.

"China Roses", Enya (Eithne Patricia Ní Bhraonáin) (1961-)

Be Free From

A young singer named Jewel recorded a wonderful song, "Life Uncommon." In it, she sings:

> *No longer lend your strength to that which you wish to be free from.*

I taught myself to play that song on my guitar, and I would often play and sing it for myself. Never for anyone else, though; I'm much too shy and self-conscious about my singing to do something so bold.

During a personal-growth seminar, specifically because it terrified me, I decided to sing "Life Uncommon" for my teammates. I practiced and practiced, wanting to make it perfect, or at least be on-key for many notes. I was a bundle of nerves as I anticipated my performance. It might have been my debut at Carnegie Hall for all the anxiety I poured into it.

And then, as I practiced the song for the 6,457th time, I stopped cold. "No longer lend your strength to that which you wish to be free from." How many times had I sung that line? I might as well have been singing in some other language because I hadn't *heard* it at all. I started to laugh. I stopped lending strength to anxiety, and it simply evaporated. (Well, mostly.)

I also thought of the end of the line: "that which you wish to *be free from*." Many songs and dreams are about freedom, even when most people reading this book enjoy freedoms unprecedented in human history. We have amazing freedom from want, harm, disease, persecution... and yet the words resonate with something in us. What do we wish to be free from?

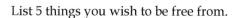

Explorations

List 5 things you wish to be free from.

Circle one at random. What will happen, or what will you have, when you are free from it?

What has to happen for you to be free from it?

We who lived in concentration camps can remember the men who walked through the huts comforting others, giving away their last piece of bread. They may have been few in number, but they offer sufficient proof that everything can be taken from a man but one thing: the last of the human freedoms — to choose one's attitude in any given set of circumstances, to choose one's own way.

Viktor Frankl (1905-1997)

Alive

We know stretching our bodies keeps us fit. Move, flex, bend, extend, twist, flow. It prevents injury, it preserves health, and it feels good. Days when I stretched my body are days I remember as energetic and satisfying. They include the days I did something new.

We know stretching our minds keeps us alert. Read, create, travel, learn a new hobby. Mind-stretches are even thought to slow or prevent mental decline as we age. Days when I stretched my mind are days I remember as full of learning. They are the days I thought something new.

What do we do to stretch our spirits? Many things quiet and soothe us: meditation, nature, gentle music, relaxing with friends. I don't mean quieting and soothing, though. What about *stretching* our spirits, stretching that part of us that is our essence? Days when I stretched my spirit, my essence, are days I remember as being *alive*. They are the days I became someone new.

As I write these words, I've been alive 18,841 days. I am a lucky man; I've enjoyed almost all of them. Yet I've felt *alive* shockingly few.

I think about the days in my life when I felt most truly alive. Getting married. Going all-out in a seminar that challenged my "I can't" assumptions. (The seminar instructor promised we would truly live that day. True.) Landing safely after an airplane engine exploded in midair. Quitting a job to start my own business. I ended all those days with a bigger view of myself than I had when those days began.

Dreams

Explorations

List 10 days when you felt truly *alive*. What did you do on those days?

List 10 things you haven't done yet and that would make you feel *alive*.

What has to happen for you to do those things?

Bonus exploration: Look around your home and notice whether or not objects in it remind you of being *alive*.

For the thirty minutes I was up there [in the cockpit after the loss of all flight controls], I was the most alive I've ever been.
That is the only way I can describe it to you.

Dennis E. Fitch (1942-), a DC-10 flight instructor, who helped land crippled United Airlines flight 232 in 1989. Of the 296 people on board, 185 survived. He was inducted into the National Aviation Hall of Fame.

Yes, it is bread we fight for — but we fight for roses, too!

"Bread and Roses," James Oppenheim (1882-1932) lyrics, Martha Coleman (?) or Caroline Kohlsaat (?), music

The world is getting to be such a dangerous place,
a man is lucky to get out of it alive.

W.C. Fields (1880-1946)

One-Way Trip

The March-April 2005 issue of Via magazine (published by the American Automobile Association) included an interview with former senator Jake Garn of Utah. He trained with NASA for six months and then spent a week on the space shuttle *Discovery* in 1985.

The reporter asked him, "Where in the cosmos will you go next?"

He said, "I'd love to be the first man on Mars — even if it's a one-way trip."

Although we may buy a one-way ticket when we move from one home to another, we know that we can buy another one-way ticket to return. Not long ago, though, searching for a better life meant permanently leaving homes, families, friends, countries, and cultures. (That's how my grand-parents came to the United States.) Today, many people make (or want to make) one-way trips to find peace, safety, or opportunity.

Earlier in *Nice Start* we noted the idea that you can have anything you want if you're willing to pay the price. Think about the prices people pay — the commitments and sacrifices, long ago and today — for their one-way trips.

Some one-way trips aren't about our position on the globe. Having children, getting divorced, or choosing a career are one-way trips.

One-way trips aren't inherently good or bad. They are simply choices, though not necessarily simple choices.

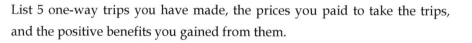

Explorations

List 5 one-way trips you have made, the prices you paid to take the trips, and the positive benefits you gained from them.

What's different about your permanent one-way trips that were worth the prices you paid and those that were not?

What would be worth a permanent one-way trip for you?

What's something you think of as a one-way trip that may not be one-way?

> *Unless commitment is made,*
> *there are only promises and hopes... but no plans.*
> Peter Drucker (1909-2005)

> *We mutually pledge to each other our lives,*
> *our fortunes, and our sacred honour.*
> Thomas Jefferson (1743-1826), the Declaration of Independence

Utopia

In college I studied the works of great political philosophers and their concepts of utopia. Their utopian ideals differed enormously, far more than the liberal-conservative conflicts we see today. I concluded that utopia depends on what we believe about human nature.

Some utopias involve government, structure, and control, because they begin with the idea that humans are nasty, brutish creatures who, if unrestrained, will rob, enslave, and kill others.

Some utopias involve dismantling social structures, because they begin with the idea that humans are loving creatures who will realize their full potential in an unconstrained state of nature.

Some utopias involve engineering new social structures based on socialization, because they begin with the idea that humans are malleable creatures who can live in harmony under the right conditions. (One philosopher in this camp thought such a utopia is possible, though it would be so different from today's society that he wouldn't want to live there.)

Utopia is not an abstract concept; it is alive in the minds of many people. Some people passionate about politics work to create a happier world. Some people passionate about religion believe that a deity will bring us (or some of us) to utopia. Many utopian communities have been built over the ages.

By the way, the word "utopia" comes from Greek in two ways. One: "eutopia", meaning the good place. The other: "outopia", meaning no place.

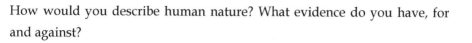

Explorations

How would you describe human nature? What evidence do you have, for and against?

What's a different concept of human nature that you think might be valid? What evidence do you have, for and against?

What would be utopia for you? Why?

Nearly all creators of Utopia have resembled the man who has toothache, and therefore thinks happiness consists in not having toothache.

George Orwell (1903-1950)

The best argument against democracy is a five-minute conversation with the average voter.

Sir Winston Churchill (1874-1965)

Dare

How dare you!

Good question. How *do* you dare? And *what* do you dare?

No, not the dares about eating some icky-gooey-ugh stuff that someone presents as a delicacy or a test of your mettle. Probably not the dares about jumping a shrieking motorcycle over a line of deadly monster trucks. Definitely not the dares about betting your life savings on a coin toss or hot-stock tip. Maybe not even the dares about asking that scrumptious human out on a date.

Not the prove-yourself, thrill-seeking, bet-it-all, why-not dares. Rather, the improve-yourself, life-seeking, get-it-all, why-I-live dares. The dares that make you (and me) tremble at their boldness even while you (and I) know they're in our hearts. The dares that wait on the other side of wistful, wishful thinking: if only I dared, maybe I could break out of my box and have the _____ (whatever it is) that would bring me true joy.

Sometimes we turn down a dare because something else is more important: we don't want to risk our family's well-being, we don't want to endanger our health, we don't want to be embarrassed, we prefer a quiet life, and so on. Sometimes, upon reflection, what seems more important may not be. Only you can honestly say what is or isn't important to you.

How dare you?

Explorations

List 5 things you have dared in your life. What do they have in common?

List 5 dares you'd have to take to get things you really want in your life. What do those dares have in common?

Imagine you are yourself 10 years in the future. What dares would future-you tell today-you to avoid? What dares to take?

Complete this sentence: "If only I dared, I would…"

Our biggest fear is not that we are inadequate.
Our deepest fear is that we are powerful beyond measure.

Marianne Williamson (1952-)

All men dream, but not equally. Those who dream by night in the dusty
recesses of their minds wake in the day to find that it was vanity:
but the dreamers of the day are dangerous men,
for they may act their dream with open eyes, to make it possible.

T.E. Lawrence (1888-1935)

Regrets

Like most of my classmates, I eagerly got right to work after I finished my MBA. I regret now that I didn't stay on to get a Ph.D or DBA.

Once upon a time there was a woman I pursued with Hollywood-style ardor, determined not to let the personal agony of a difficult courtship keep us from our Hollywood-style happy ending. When it became clear that I was a supporting actor playing the role of the suitor-who-loses, I sadly accepted the outcome. No regrets, though, because I knew that I'd given the pursuit all I had.

Who knows how my life would have felt with the degree or the woman? Maybe I'd have been bored silly with a career in academia, or maybe I'd have contributed some earth-shaking discovery. (Maybe I still will.) Maybe I'd have been unhappy sharing life with that woman, or maybe I would have been with her like my uncle Eli and aunt Jennie, who were lovebirds into their 80s. (Maybe I still will, with a different woman.)

I faced a painful choice some years ago. Meanwhile, my best friend, a man I'd known since fifth grade, was dying of leukemia. His last words to me, 3 days before he died, were "Don't spend your life making up your mind." (Thank you, my friend.) We never know what lies down the paths we don't take. My regrets come only from letting myself be blown off course or led down paths, instead of making up my mind and choosing my own.

Explorations

What are 3 things you will regret if you don't do them (or stop doing them)?

Circle the potential regret that makes your eyes mist up the most. What are 3 steps you can take to prevent that potential regret?

Circle the step(s) you will take today.

If that plane leaves the ground and you're not with him, you'll regret it. Maybe not today. Maybe not tomorrow, but soon and for the rest of your life.

Rick Blaine (Humphrey Bogart, 1899-1957) to Ilsa Lund (Ingrid Bergman, 1915-1982) in *Casablanca* (1942)

The time has come for me to ... kick off my shoes, and speak my piece. 'The days of struggle are over,' I should be able to say. 'I can look back now and tell myself I don't have a single regret.' But I do. Many years ago a very wise man named Bernard Baruch took me aside and put his arm around my shoulder. 'Harpo, my boy,' he said, 'I'm going to give you three pieces of advice, three things you should always remember.' My heart jumped and I glowed with expectation. I was going to hear the magic password to a rich, full life from the master himself. 'Yes, sir?' I said. And he told me the three things. I regret that I've forgotten what they were.

Arthur/Adolph (Harpo) Marx (1888-1964)

Success

Here are some ways that people define success:

> Money. Fame. Beauty. Survival. Long life. Freedom. Free time. Children. Marriage. Possessions. Piety. Serenity. High test scores. Being first. Being well-adjusted. Being loved. Loving. Working. Achieving a goal. Setting a record. Overcoming fear. Overcoming handicaps. Great effort. Great decisions. Great results. The journey. Applause. Inner satisfaction. Health. Time to relax. Parties!

Success involves tradeoffs. For instance, achieving great works and taking time to relax can be in conflict. For another instance, you probably will find it difficult to pursue everything. You've got to choose what you really want.

Success implies measurement. Is it success to score 500 (on a scale of 200 to 800) on the verbal portion of the SAT? Maybe yes for the immigrant who didn't speak English six months ago. Maybe no for the child of sixth-generation English professors who piped the works of Shakespeare, Dickens, and Marx (Groucho) into the crib.

Success requires value judgments. There is no universally "right" way to measure success. Cultures differ dramatically in how they define success, and so do individuals within a culture. However, if you don't define success for yourself, then you will use someone else's definition and you will find it difficult to know when (or if) you have achieved it.

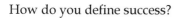

Explorations

How do you define success?

Does your definition require being better or doing better than other people?

If you are not successful according to your definition, are you a failure?

Would you want the people you love to use your definition of success?

Like almost everyone who uses e-mail, I receive a ton of spam every day.
Much of it offers to help me get out of debt or get rich quick.
It would be funny if it weren't so exciting.

Bill Gates (1955-)

The common idea that success spoils people by making them vain, egotistic
and self-complacent is erroneous; on the contrary it makes them,
for the most part, humble, tolerant, and kind.

W. Somerset Maugham (1874-1965)

A rich man eats when he wishes / A poor man, whenever he can.

"Rich Man, Poor Man", words and music by Peter Yarrow (1938-)
and Peter Zimmel (?)

Time's Up

It breaks my heart to write this true sentence: As I write these words, my beloved mother has been dead for 3 days.

Sometimes we remind ourselves of life's brevity with a cute phrase such as "today is the first day of the rest of your life." Sometimes we use the fatalistic "you never know." Sometimes we acknowledge that someone else's departure will eventually be ours: "There but for fortune go I."

I imagine a grand clock that softly, firmly, finally strikes "time's up."

When she went to sleep one night, my mother didn't know her clock would strike before she woke up. I don't know when mine will. You don't know when yours will. All we know is that each of us will reach time's up.

We are aware of our mortality and of our desire, our hunger, even our ache to do certain things before our time's up.

Got time?

I want to be thoroughly used up when I die,
for the harder I work the more I live. I rejoice in life for its own sake.
George Bernard Shaw (1856-1950)

Explorations

This book is not the first to encourage a reader to do what he or she really wants to do, and this exploration is not the only one in this book on that subject. Then again, we can hardly claim to have made a nice start if we don't define the happy ending.

What will you do before your time's up? Think about what you want to see, hear, taste, touch, or smell. Think about what you want to discard, regain, or be free from. Think about what you want to give, receive, create, achieve, enjoy, learn, teach, build, fix, read, write, say, sing, or love. (Few people want to destroy or hate more before their time's up.) Be specific. Focus on action: "I will find my true love," versus "I want to be in love."

1. _____

2. _____

3. _____

4. _____

5. _____

6. _____

7. _____

8. _____

9. _____

10. _____

11. _____

12. _____

13. _____

14. _____

15. _____

16. _____

17. _____

18. _____

19. _____

20. _____

21. _____

22. _____

Dreams

23. _____

24. _____

25. _____

26. _____

27. _____

28. _____

29. _____

30. _____

31. _____

32. _____

33. _____

34. _____

35. _____

36. _____

37. _____

38. _____

39. _____

40. _____

41. _____

42. _____

43. _____

44. _____

45. _____

46. _____

47. _____

48. _____

49. _____

50. _____

Dreams

51. _____

52. _____

53. _____

54. _____

55. _____

56. _____

57. _____

58. _____

59. _____

60. _____

61. _____

62. _____

63. _____

64. _____

65. _____

66. _____

67. _____

68. _____

69. _____

70. _____

71. _____

72. _____

73. _____

74. _____

75. _____

76. _____

77. _____

78. _____

Dreams

79. _____

80. _____

81. _____

82. _____

83. _____

84. _____

85. _____

86. _____

87. _____

88. _____

89. _____

90. _____

91. _____

92. _____

93. _____

94. _____

95. _____

96. _____

97. _____

98. _____

99. _____

100._____

Add more pages as needed.

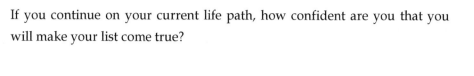

If you continue on your current life path, how confident are you that you will make your list come true?

What did you leave off your list? Why?

What will you do (or stop doing) to make your list come true?

List 5 reasons why you deserve the things on your list.

List 5 more.

Don't get called out on strikes.
Leo Durocher (?) (1906-1991)

Have the courage to live. Anyone can die.
Robert Cody (?)

No one can go back and start a new beginning,
but anyone can start today and make a new ending.
Maria Robinson (?)

Tigers

The master spoke to the disciple. "There are two tigers within me, and they are fighting."

"Master, which tiger will win?," asked the disciple.

The master responded, "Whichever one I feed."

The tigers within me that fight most viciously are those named fear (of failure and looking stupid) and excitement (about moving forward and making a difference). Their conflict showed up starkly for me as I wrote this book.

I feel vulnerable wondering whether you'll favorably judge what I've written. This book isn't a report with well-researched facts and figures; it is a collection of personal thoughts, insights, reminiscences, and ideas, close to my heart. Will you be moved, will you be impressed, will you be vaguely amused, will you think I am a pompous fool? How will I feel if I keep the book hidden inside me? How will I feel when I see it in print?

Which tiger did I feed? Well, you are holding this book.

Explorations

List 3 areas in your life where you feel torn in different directions. Those are areas where your tigers are fighting.

Circle the one where the fighting feels most intense.

What are the names of the fiercest tigers fighting there?

What are you doing to feed each tiger?

Nice Start

What It's All About

We've come a long way, dear reader, you and I. Let's review and resolve. Review, look again; resolve, come to a conclusion; resolve, commit to act.

In *Yourself* you explored who you are and who you want to be. You defined success and identified the traits that live at your core. You questioned what and how you choose to believe. You connected with Marlon Brando.

In *Others* you explored yourself relative to those baffling, irrational, stereotyped people who take up space around you. You thought about what they think about, the promises you exchange, the roles you play, how close you and they are, and the many people for whom you are thankful.

In *Perspectives* you flipped things around and took a different look. You explored numbers, messages, casinos, progress, and things we know that ain't so. You thought about great truths and life, and getting a D.

In *Dreams* you explored the tomorrow you hope for, aspire to, set goals to achieve, and fantasize about. Dreams about briefcases, one-way trips, and utopia. Tomorrows and regrets, tigers, and eventually time's up.

It all adds up to who you are, who you want to be, and who you will be.

Maybe you had a few surprises along the way. Maybe you'll have more as you continue to explore, as I do. Maybe you developed some answers. And maybe things look a little different to you, as they do for me.

That, for me, is the payoff. Things look a little different. That means new ideas, new clarity, new opportunities, new action, conscious action. All of which adds up to knowing better what I want, knowing better how to achieve what I want, and living the life that I want.

And you see why I disregarded the advice of the people who, after reading drafts of the book, said I should tell you what to do. I don't have your answers. How could I? The hundreds of questions in this book are about values, preferences, beliefs, and goals. They're personal. For me to tell you how you should answer those questions would be like me pressing my great truths on you: enjoy Beethoven and avoid beets at all costs.

The meaning of life, or at least the meaning of *Nice Start*, is not Beethoven good, beets bad. What it's all about is honesty and openness with yourself. What it's all about is pursuing your goals and joy with as much sincerity as you wish others would pursue their goals and joy.

It is by thinking in that spirit about the questions in this book, and by adopting the gently inquiring style I hope I have demonstrated in this book, that I have found answers for myself. (Not all of them; I'm not done yet.) So, although I don't have your answers, I hope I have helped you find them. As I have found inspiration and direction for action in my life, I hope you do too.

In that spirit of honesty and openness, I'd like to share one last thought with you about what *Nice Start* means to me.

"Legend," a CD by Steve McDonald, has a song called "The Queen and the Rhymer." It tells the story of Thomas the Rhymer and his journey to Fairyland after he met and fell in love with its queen. He was sent back to earth with a special gift:

> *With gifts of truth his wisdom and poetry sang*

Seven years later, he returned to Fairyland and his love:

> *There he remained never heard from again*
> *Yet the song of the rhymer still lingers on.*

Nice Start is my modest wisdom and poetry. Someday I will never be heard from again... and I hope you like my song enough to let it linger with you.

Final exploration

Give your gifts of wisdom, and sing your song.

All the Days of Your Life

I'm an eager, enthusiastic guy and I'm not always patient. I want everything to happen *now*. With a single click of the mouse you can do anything! (Never mind how many clicks preceded that single click.)

When I started down the path that led to this book, I began acquiring new concepts, tools, thoughts, and perspectives. I found that even though I embraced them wholeheartedly and they made a positive difference right away, it takes more than a single click to replace old habits and thinking. And, being human rather than a god or robot, I found that sometimes I slip.

You've started down a new path. Give yourself time. Relax. Open. Read. Stretch. Listen. Think. Don't judge by what's easy or popular; go for what's good and true. Change. Respect your process, celebrate your progress. Be compassionate with yourself. Take action, and be conscious of which tigers you feed.

You've reached the end of *Nice Start,* and you're beginning your own nice start. In keeping with that 2-word spirit, here's one more question:

What's next?

Thank you for joining me.

> *May you live all the days of your life.*
> Jonathan Swift (1667-1745)

Appendix

Appendix

Further Reading

A Devil's Chaplain, Richard Dawkins

Beyond Freedom and Dignity, B.F. Skinner

Decision Traps, J. Edward Russo and Paul J.H. Schoemaker

Flim-Flam!, James Randi

Fooled By Randomness, Nassim Nicholas Taleb

How Would You Move Mount Fuji?, William Poundstone

Innumeracy, John Allen Paulos

Judgment in Managerial Decision Making, Max H. Bazerman

Living a Life That Matters, Harold S. Kushner

Man's Search For Meaning, Viktor Frankl

Mistakes Were Made (but not by me), Carol Tavris and Elliot Aronson

Story People, Brian Andreas

The Autobiography of Mark Twain, Mark Twain (duh)

The Culture of Fear, Barry Glassner

The Diaries of Adam and Eve, Mark Twain

The Drunkard's Walk, Leonard Mlodinow

The Logic of Failure, Dietrich Dörner

The Lucifer Effect, Philip Zimbardo

The Psychology of Judgment and Decision Making, Scott Plous

Why Not?, Barry Nalebuff and Ian Ayres

Women Can't Hear What Men Don't Say, Warren Farrell

The man who does not read books
has no advantage over the man that cannot read them.
Mark Twain (1835-1910)

About the Author

Mark Chussil is Founder and CEO of Advanced Competitive Strategies, Inc. He was designed ACS's award-winning ValueWar® strategy simulator. He is also a Founder of Crisis Simulations International, LLC, and inventor of the DXMA™ crisis simulator (U.S. Patent No. 7,536,287).

Mark speaks at conferences around the world about how strategists can make much better business decisions. He has published a book and numerous articles, and contributed chapters and case studies to five other books, on decision-making, competitive strategy, and crisis planning.

Born and raised in New Haven, Connecticut, Mark earned his B.A. with an Intensive Major in Political Science at Yale. He focused on political philosophy, in particular the concept of utopia. He planned to become a professor of political science, consciously switched to business, and earned an M.B.A. at Harvard. With a little help from his friends at The Strategic Planning Institute, he learned about business, public speaking, statistics and writing software.

After 16 years in Boston, Mark moved to Oregon, where he has lived since 1990.

Mark took his first personal-effectiveness seminar in 1999, and it was life-changing. He has avidly followed that path through other seminars, including risking his life (not really) climbing and jumping off a telephone pole. It was hard. It was a pole.

Mark has traveled extensively, and has visited every continent except Antarctica. His favorite places so far include Cape Town, Jackson (New Hampshire), London, Tuscany, Venice, and the west coast of the USA. He loves cross-country skiing, fine wines, movies, fitness, photography, and museums. He plays his guitar and sings when he thinks no one else can hear.

A positive attitude may not solve all your problems,
but it will annoy enough people to make it worth the effort.

Herm Albright (1876-1944)

A mind forever voyaging through strange seas of thought, alone.

William Wordsworth (1770-1850)

Go confidently in the direction of your dreams
Live the life you have imagined.

Henry David Thoreau (1817-1862)

Index of People Mentioned

Appendix

Mother Teresa, 74

Nalebuff, Barry, 180

Newton, Sir Isaac, 30

Nietzsche, Friedrich, 33

Oppenheim, James, 147

Orwell, George, 151

Palmer, Arnold, 26

Paulos, John Allen, ix, 116, 179

Picard, Captain, i

Plato, 65, 111

Player, Gary, 26

Plous, Scott, ix, 86, 180

Pope, Alexander, 20

Poundstone, William, 179

Proverb (Chinese), 97

Proverb (Japanese), 74

Queen Elizabeth, 61

Randi, James, 179

Rappaport, Herbert, 134

Republicans, 48, 68

Rice, Tim, 129

Robertson, Nan, 62

Robinson, Maria, 167

Rogers, Will, 121

Roosevelt, Eleanor, 109

Roosevelt, Theodore, 129

Russo, J. Edward, ix, 179

Sagan, Carl, 101

Schoemaker, Paul J.H., ix, 179

Shakespeare, William, 23, 105, 156

Shaw, George Bernard, 61, 99, 158

Simon, William E., 109

Skinner, B.F., 179

Southard, John E., 79

Swift, Jonathan, 52, 175

Taleb, Nassim Nicholas, 179

Tavris, Carol, ix, 68, 113, 179

Thiagarajan, Sivasailam (Thiagi), v

Thoreau, Henry David, 182

Twain, Mark, 19, 83, 96, 121, 138, 143, 179, 180

Unknown, 28, 39, 75, 101

Vidal, Gore, 72

Warhol, Andy, 141

Washington, George, 103

Watterson, Bill, 132

Wayne, John, 115

Webber, Sir Andrew Lloyd, 132

Wells, H.G., 66

Wiesel, Elie, 126

Wilder, Thornton, 57

Williams, Donald, 124

Williamson, Marianne, 153

Wordsworth, William, 182

CPSIA information can be obtained
at www.ICGtesting.com
Printed in the USA
LVOW04s0414081215

465787LV00036B/1673/P